ATLAS OF CONFLICTS

THE
KOREAN
WAR

Reg Grant

W
FRANKLIN WATTS
LONDON•SYDNEY

Titles in this series:
THE ARAB-ISRAELI CONFLICT
THE KOREAN WAR
THE VIETNAM WAR
WORLD WAR I
WORLD WAR II: EUROPE
WORLD WAR II: THE PACIFIC

© 2004 Arcturus Publishing Ltd

Produced for Franklin Watts by Arcturus Publishing Ltd, 26/27 Bickels Yard, 151-153 Bermondsey Street, London SE1 3HA.

Series concept: Alex Woolf
Editor: Philip de Ste. Croix
Designer: Simon Borrough
Cartography: The Map Studio
Consultant: Paul Cornish, Imperial War Museum, London
Picture researcher: Thomas Mitchell

Published in the UK by Franklin Watts.

A CIP catalogue record for this book is available from the British Library.

ISBN 0 7496 5451 1

Printed and bound in Italy

Franklin Watts – the Watts Publishing Group, 96 Leonard Street, London EC2A 4XD.

Picture Acknowledgements:
All the photographs in this book were supplied by Getty Images and are reproduced here with their permission.

ABOUT THE AUTHOR

The author, Reg Grant, studied history at the University of Oxford, and is the author of more than twenty books on modern history. He specializes in the history of the twentieth century. His book *The Holocaust* (1997) was shortlisted for the *Times Educational Supplement*'s Senior Information Book Award.

CONTENTS

CHAPTER 1:
FROM ONE WAR TO THE NEXT

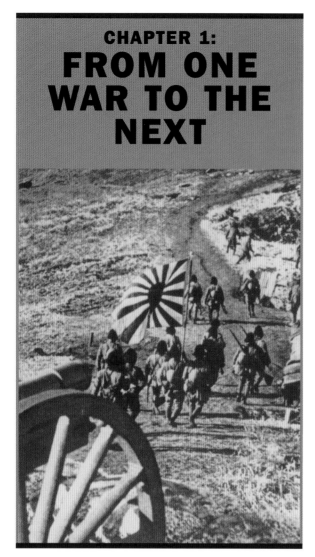

Japanese forces advance into Manchuria in 1931, setting Japan on the path to World War II.

At the start of the twentieth century, Korea was a unified, independent kingdom. It had been ruled by the Yi dynasty for over 500 years. In 1910, however, the country was taken over by its powerful neighbour, Japan. The Japanese ruled Korea as a colony and did their best to wipe out Koreans' sense of national identity. The Japanese language was used for business, government and higher education. Only a minority of Koreans who collaborated with the Japanese benefited from their rule.

In the 1930s Japan set out to expand its empire in Asia. In 1931 the Japanese occupied Manchuria, across Korea's northern border, and then moved further into China, where full-scale war broke out in 1937. Japan's expansion brought it into confrontation with the United States, which backed China's Nationalist leader, Chiang Kai-shek. In December 1941 the Japanese went to war with the United States and Britain, launching World War II in the Pacific. A series of swift military victories allowed Japan to occupy a large area of Asia, including the Philippines, Malaysia and Indonesia. But the tide of war soon turned, and by 1945 Japan was facing total defeat at the hands of the United States and its allies.

AMERICA'S ALLIES
One of America's allies in World War II was the Soviet Union, ruled by the communist dictator Joseph Stalin. Between 1939 and 1941 the Soviets had fought a war with Japan on the border between Manchuria and the Soviet Union. But the two countries then agreed a neutrality pact, and from 1941 to 1945 the Soviets were not at war with Japan, even though they were allies of the United States and Britain in their war against Germany. The Soviet Union did eventually declare war on Japan, but not until 8 August 1945 – two days after the Americans dropped the first atom bomb on the Japanese city of Hiroshima. By the time Japan surrendered on 15 August, Soviet troops had invaded Manchuria and had advanced into the far north of Korea.

THE JAPANESE SURRENDER
In the final days before the Japanese surrender, the Americans hurried to devise a plan for the occupation of Korea by

SOVIET INTEREST

In March 1946 the head of the Soviet delegation to a joint US-Soviet commission on Korean reunification said:
'The Soviet Union has a keen interest in Korea being a true ... independent country, friendly to the Soviet Union, so that in future it will not become a base for an attack on the Soviet Union.'
[Quoted in *Rethinking the Korean War*, William Stueck]

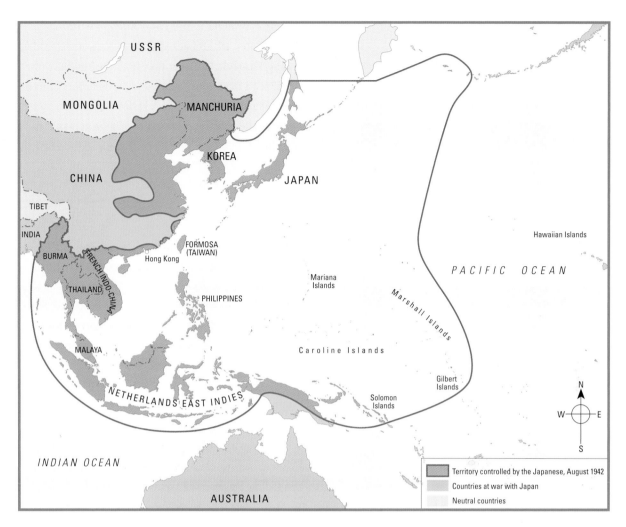

At its greatest extent during World War II, Japan's empire included most of East and South-east Asia. Korea had been Japan's first conquest, formally taken over back in 1910.

the victorious Allies. Military advisers to the US president, Harry S. Truman, drew up a proposal to divide Korea into two zones, with Soviet troops occupying the area north of the 38th parallel and American troops the area south of that line. Stalin accepted the proposal and Soviet troops, commanded by General Ivan Chistiakov, rapidly spread out through their zone. American troops began to arrive in Korea a few weeks later to occupy the south. The American occupation

President Harry S. Truman (centre) holds up the document signed by the Japanese when they surrendered to the Allies in 1945.

Korean students welcome US troops arriving to occupy the south of their country in autumn 1945.

force was commanded by General John R. Hodge.

In brief discussions on Korea during World War II, the Soviets and Americans had broadly agreed that the Koreans would not be ready to rule themselves when the Japanese were removed. The United States proposed that Korea should spend some years under foreign 'trusteeship' before being accorded full independence. Most Koreans, by contrast, expected their country to regain its independence immediately after the Japanese defeat. By the time US troops began to arrive, some political groups in the Korean capital, Seoul, had already declared an independent 'Korean People's Republic'. Throughout the country, Koreans had set up 'people's committees' to run affairs at local level. But neither the Americans nor the Soviets intended to let the Koreans sort out their own future, and both occupation zones came under the military rule of the two foreign powers.

LIVING IN EXILE Many Koreans who actively opposed Japanese rule had been forced to live in exile, some in the Soviet Union, some in China, and

Residents of Seoul, Korea's largest city, make the victory sign to celebrate the defeat of Japan.

In 1945 Korea was occupied by Soviet forces north of the 38th parallel and by the Americans south of it. The 38th parallel was just a line on a map – it cut across many roads and railways.

some in the United States. After the Japanese defeat, these exiles returned to their home country, with different ideas about how it should be run. The Americans and the Soviets each quickly found a former exile to back as Korea's future leader. In October 1945, General Hodge welcomed the return to Korea of Syngman Rhee, a 70-year-old Korean nationalist who had lived in the United States for a quarter of a century. The Soviets, for their part, chose to back Kim Il-sung, a 33-year-old Korean communist who had fought in a guerrilla war against the Japanese in Manchuria in the 1930s and had then spent most of World War II in the Soviet Union.

Neither the Soviets nor the Americans at first intended to divide Korea in two. But each of the two great powers wanted Korea to be united under a government favourable to itself. The chances of agreement being reached in Korea faded as the wider relationship between the Soviet Union and the United States grew worse. In 1947, President Truman declared the 'Truman Doctrine', committing the United States to

Soviet dictator Joseph Stalin wanted to spread communist influence, but without involving his country in a war with the United States.

Korea, each side built up a political system in the area under its military control. North of the 38th parallel, a Soviet-style state was constructed, with power concentrated in the hands of the communist North Korean Workers' Party. Most key positions were held by Koreans who, like Kim Il-sung, had recently returned from the Soviet Union. Soviet forces withdrew from Korea in 1948 and the area north of the 38th parallel became independent as the Democratic People's Republic of Korea (DPRK), with Kim Il-sung as president. Although there were some local revolts against communist rule, the Soviet-installed regime was largely secure in its control of North Korea.

SOUTH OF THE 38TH PARALLEL

South of the 38th parallel, events did not go as smoothly. The Americans forcibly suppressed the 'people's committees', which they regarded as hot-beds of communism, and found themselves relying upon administrators and police who had formerly worked for the Japanese. Political life was chaotic, marked by local revolts, violent action by armed political extremist groups, and assassinations.

In 1948 Rhee won elections supervised by the United Nations, and became president of the Republic of Korea (ROK). But Rhee's control of the South was nothing like as secure as Kim's in

opposing the spread of communism worldwide. By 1949 the Americans and Soviets were open enemies, confronting one another in the 'Cold War'.

In the absence of agreement on the unification of

YOSU REBELLION

During the guerrilla war in South Korea, government forces had to suppress an uprising in the port of Yosu in October 1948. Official estimates of casualties in this operation were:

South Korean soldiers dead or missing	404
Rebels killed	821
Rebels captured	2,860
Civilians killed	over 1,000

the North. He soon faced a major guerrilla uprising, starting on the island of Cheju-do and then spreading to the Korean mainland. The North Koreans supported the anti-Rhee guerrillas in the South, just as the South Koreans promoted guerrilla activity, on a much smaller scale, in the North. The ROK authorities, with the aid of American advisers, had largely suppressed the guerrilla movement by early 1950, but only through ruthless action that cost tens of thousands of lives.

The ROK and the DPRK both strongly claimed to rule the whole of Korea. From the early summer of 1949 onward there were clashes along the 38th parallel between the forces of the two Koreas, bent on testing one another's defences. By June 1950, it has been estimated that up to 100,000 Koreans had died in guerrilla fighting and border clashes – victims of what has been called a 'Korean Civil War'. Both Kim and Rhee were eager to mount a full-scale invasion across

Kim Il-Sung, leader of North Korea from 1948, had a burning ambition to unite all of Korea under communist rule.

Between 1948 and early 1950, guerrillas backed by North Korea fought against South Korean government forces on the island of Cheju-do and across mountainous areas of the mainland. At the same time, South Korea promoted guerrilla activity inside North Korea.

the 38th parallel, each confident that he would emerge as the ruler of a unified Korea. Until 1950, however, neither could obtain permission for such a move from their powerful backers, the Soviet Union or the United States.

AMERICA'S CAUTION   The United States had no desire to support a military adventure that might bring war with the Soviet Union. America's political leaders had an uneasy relationship with Rhee, feeling suspicious of his aggressive nationalism. Stalin was equally unready for a 'hot war' with the United States. The Soviets doubted Kim's ability to conquer the South, and they feared that an invasion would provoke the Americans into sending troops back into Korea.

ON A VOLCANO'S EDGE

Harold J. Noble, first secretary at the US Embassy in South Korea in 1950, claimed that America's failure to foresee a North Korean invasion was the result of living too long 'on the edge of a volcano'. He wrote:

'We knew it would explode some day, but as day after day, month after month, and year after year passed and it did not blow up, we could hardly believe that tomorrow would be any different.'

[Quoted in *Rethinking the Korean War*, William Stueck]

The promise of support from Communist China made it possible for North Korea to invade the South. Here, a Chinese student who has volunteered to fight in Korea is given a rousing send-off.

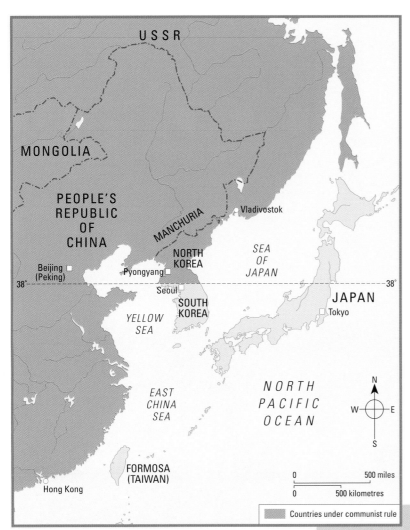

zone – a fact carefully noted by the Soviet Union.

Mao's victory seems to have changed Stalin's view of the Korean situation. In January 1950 the Soviet leader agreed to supply Kim Il-sung with the heavy armaments that he had long requested. The following April, the Soviets told Kim that he could attack the South if he got the backing of the Chinese – it was made clear to him that he could not expect the Soviet Union to intervene on his behalf if things went wrong. In May, Mao agreed to support Kim's proposed military action, promising Chinese military support if needed. The way was open for a North Korean invasion of South Korea.

The communist victory in China left South Korea the only non-communist state in mainland East Asia.

The international situation changed dramatically, however, in October 1949. In that month, in China, the forces of Mao Tse-tung, the leader of the Chinese Communist Party, achieved a decisive victory in their Civil War against the Nationalist forces of Chiang Kai-shek, and a communist People's Republic was proclaimed in Beijing, China's capital. The remaining Nationalist forces took refuge on the island of Formosa (Taiwan), which lay about 200 km to the east of China. Mao signed an alliance with the Soviet Union in February 1950.

The Chinese communist victory inevitably focused American attention on East Asia. Korea, however, was still far from America's main concern. In a speech in January 1950 US Secretary of State Dean Acheson left it out of a list of countries that the United States regarded as within its 'defensive perimeter' in the eastern Pacific

Chiang Kai-shek, leader of the Chinese Nationalists who were defeated by the communists in 1949.

CHAPTER 2:
THE KOREAN WAR ERUPTS

The Korean War began at 4.00 am on Sunday, 25 June 1950. After a preparatory artillery barrage, troops of the North Korean People's Army (NKPA) attacked South Korean positions on the Ongjin peninsula, on Korea's west coast. Through the morning the North Korean offensive spread eastward along the 320-km length of the 38th parallel, with thrusts towards Kaesong, Uijongbu, Chunchon, and down the east coast.

An arbitrary line on a map, the 38th parallel was not a defensible border – it followed no natural feature such as a river or mountain range. Also, the invasion achieved almost total surprise. Many South Korean officers and all but one US military adviser were away from frontline units, enjoying a weekend's leave. Kaesong was occupied within hours almost without a fight. There was some stiff South Korean resistance, especially at Chunchon, where the defenders had

Two days after the start of the war, a newspaper seller in London reports the bad news from Korea.

Soviet T-34 tanks were among the World War II-vintage equipment used by the North Koreans.

US ARMY NUMBERS

Sharply reduced in numbers after World War II, the US Army had to expand rapidly to meet the demands of the war in Korea:

	US Army strength
July 1946	1,891,000 (including Army Air Force)
June 1950	591,000
July 1953	1,530,000

untypically been on the alert for an attack. But in general the North Koreans made rapid progress.

On paper the North Korean and South Korean armed forces were of equal strength, both numbering around 95,000. But the North Korean forces included thousands of battle-hardened troops and experienced officers who had fought on the communist side in the recent civil war in China. Others had served in the Soviet Red Army. They were equipped with good World War II-vintage Soviet equipment, including about 150 T-34 tanks. The South Koreans were in general poorly trained and equipped. They had no tanks and poor anti-tank weapons.

NORTH KOREANS REACH SEOUL

Within three days of the start of the invasion, North Korean troops had reached Seoul, the capital of South Korea. Retreating southward from the city, the South Koreans in panic blew up bridges over the Han River too soon, killing hundreds of civilian refugees and soldiers who were still crossing the river and leaving many of their own troops and essential supplies stranded on the wrong side.

The North Korean government presented its military action as a legitimate response to a 'general attack' by the South Koreans across the 38th parallel. The United States and its allies, by contrast, denounced the North Korean invasion as – in the words of British Prime Minister Clement Attlee – an act of 'naked aggression'. The Americans had no hesitation about intervening militarily in support of

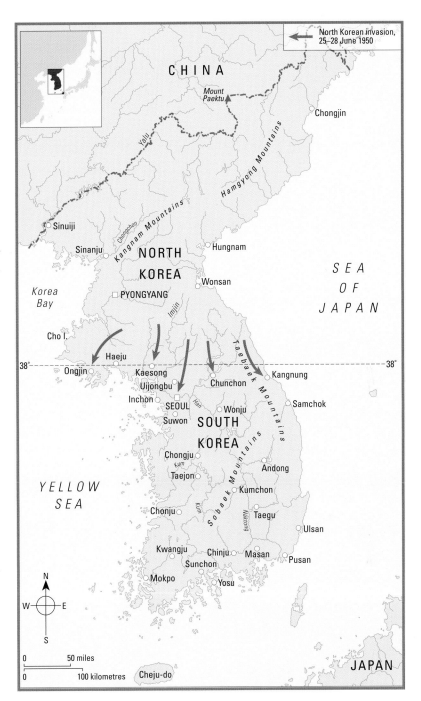

The first North Korean attack on 25 June 1950 was in the west, at Ongjin. Kaesong was soon occupied by the invaders, but they met stiffer resistance in front of Chunchon. The most important thrust was towards Seoul, which fell to the communists on 28 June.

the ROK. President Truman authorized air strikes against the North Koreans and the US Navy's Task Force 77 was ordered to sail into position to blockade the Korean coast. There was serious discussion among US political and military leaders about whether they

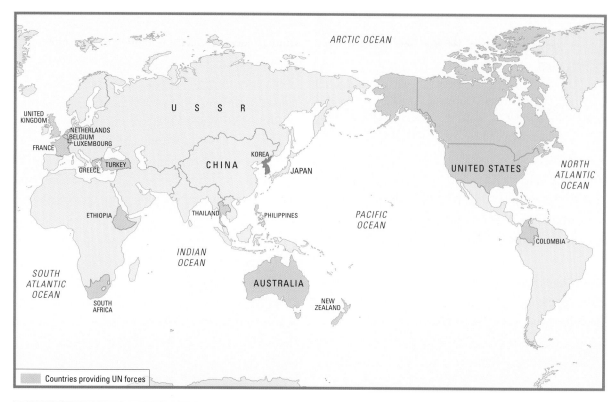

Countries providing UN forces

General Douglas MacArthur (right) is briefed by a staff officer in Korea, September 1950.

After the United States, Britain made the largest contribution to UN forces. Australia, Canada, New Zealand, Turkey, Colombia, Philippines and Thailand also provided substantial contingents. France, embroiled in a war in Indo-China, sent only a token force.

should use nuclear weapons to halt the invasion.

The US Commander in the Far East, General Douglas MacArthur, was based in Japan, which was then still under US military occupation. On 29 June, MacArthur flew to Suwon airfield, south of Seoul, to assess the situation for himself. Seeing the disorganized ROK troops in full retreat, MacArthur decided that US ground forces would be needed to turn back the communist advance. On 30 June President Truman authorized the dispatch of US troops to South Korea. The first units arrived there from Japan the following day.

UN DIPLOMATIC ACTIVITY Meanwhile, the outbreak of war in Korea had triggered frantic diplomatic activity. The Americans saw the invasion as part of a worldwide communist strategy directed by the Soviet Union against the 'free world'. The governments of the United States' friends and allies,

Immediately after news of the invasion broke, the United States presented a resolution to the United Nations Security Council demanding an immediate North Korean withdrawal to the 38th parallel. The Soviet Union, a permanent member of the Security Council, could have vetoed acceptance of this resolution. But the Soviets were boycotting the Council over the issue of Chinese representation – the Chinese Nationalists continued to represent China at the UN despite their defeat by the communists. In the absence of the Soviet Union, the Security Council backed the resolution. On 27 June, a second resolution was passed calling on UN member states to take collective military action in support of South Korea. Early in July, another resolution determined that forces from UN member states sent to Korea would operate under a Unified Command provided by the United States. MacArthur became commander of UN Forces in Korea.

including Britain, did not all fully accept this view, but they did agree that North Korea had been guilty of armed aggression. Under the charter of the United Nations Organization, set up at the end of World War II, any country that carried out an act of aggression was supposed to be resisted by joint action on the part of UN members, who had jointly agreed to uphold world peace.

The involvement of the United Nations gave an international seal of approval to US military intervention in Korea, but its practical effect was

A military band greets an American troopship arriving at the Korean port of Pusan in late July 1950. Holding Pusan was essential for the UN forces if reinforcements and heavy equipment were to be brought in.

British troops from the colony of Hong Kong embark to join the UN forces in Korea, 25 August 1950. US troops had been in Korea since July.

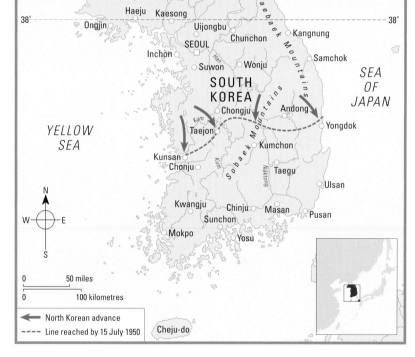

limited. US commanders in Korea continued to operate under the US president and US chiefs of staff – there was no question of them taking orders from UN Secretary-General Trygve Lie. And although Britain and some British Commonwealth countries quickly sent naval and/or airforce units to fight in the Korean theatre, initially only American troops joined the ROK forces in the ground war.

The US Army was not well prepared for a ground war. Since the end of World War II it had experienced sharp cuts in funding and troop numbers. As the only country in the world in possession of atom bombs (at least until 1949), the US had felt it could rely on those nuclear weapons for national defence, without spending heavily on

After the fall of Seoul on 28 June the US military headquarters in Korea was moved from Suwon to Taejon. The first US troops to arrive were ordered to block the road south from Suwon, but the North Korean advance swept them aside. By 15 July the North Koreans were on the outskirts of Taejon and threatening Yongdok on the east coast.

conventional weapons or on training men to fight. Nevertheless, US military leaders entered the war with a confident belief that they could easily defeat the North Koreans. MacArthur planned for his men to retake Inchon, the major port nearest to Seoul, within three weeks.

Instead of powering their way to an easy victory, however, the Americans soon found themselves engaged in a desperate struggle to avoid a humiliating defeat. The first US troops hurriedly sent to Korea on 1 July 1950 were known as 'Task Force Smith', after their commander Lieutenant Colonel 'Brad' Smith. Positioned across the road south from Suwon with orders to delay the NKPA advance, they were routed by a North Korean column on 5 July. The same fate befell other US infantry formations brought over from Japan and thrown into the front line. Ill-prepared for combat after peaceful years as an occupation force, they were outfought and outmanoeuvred by the North Koreans who were superior in morale and fighting skill. South Korean guerrilla fighters, who had survived the suppression of their campaign against Rhee in 1948-50, also harassed the Americans and ROK forces. Operating behind the front, the guerrillas cut supply lines and ambushed isolated patrols.

Fighting a series of delaying actions, the Americans fell back on Taejon. There fierce street fighting took place before the city was abandoned on 20 July, with the US divisional commander, General William F. Dean, falling prisoner to the North Koreans. By the end of July, the whole of western South Korea had been lost to the NKPA and the American and ROK forces were withdrawing towards the key port of Pusan. Their hope now was to hold a defensive perimeter around the port until sufficient reinforcements arrived to mount a counterattack. The North Koreans, meanwhile, although severely battered by US air strikes and stiffening US resistance on the ground, continued to press forward, sensing that victory was almost in their grasp.

General William F. Dean led the defence of Taejon. Trapped behind enemy lines when the city fell, he was later taken prisoner.

CHAPTER 3:
THE TABLES TURNED

An American tank defends a position near Masan, on the Pusan perimeter. The arrival of tanks in August 1950 helped halt the North Korean advance.

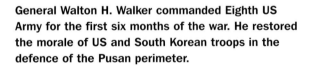

General Walton H. Walker commanded Eighth US Army for the first six months of the war. He restored the morale of US and South Korean troops in the defence of the Pusan perimeter.

At the beginning of August 1950, the Americans and ROK were still struggling to stabilize a defensive perimeter around the port of Pusan. A North Korean column was advancing on Masan, near the south coast of Korea, within 50 km of Pusan. Lieutenant General Walton H. Walker, the commander of what was now known as the Eighth US Army in Korea, threw the newly arrived 1st Marine Brigade into the battle to block this advance. More than 6,000 strong, equipped with Pershing tanks that outgunned the Soviet-supplied T-34s, the Marines were a different proposition from the mostly ill-equipped and inexperienced US infantry the North Koreans had

previously fought. The attacking column was thrown back with heavy losses.

General Walker made it plain to his men that no further withdrawals were to be permitted. The defensive perimeter he established measured roughly 130 km from north to south and 80 km from east to west. The perimeter was not a continuous barrier but a line of strongpoints. Its defence depended on the swift movement of troops to reinforce areas that came under pressure.

THE PERIMETER HOLDS   For six weeks, from the start of August to mid-September, battle raged along the perimeter, switching from sector to sector as the North Korean forces, commanded by General Kim Chaik, sought a decisive breakthrough. There was a critical period at the eastern end of the perimeter in the second week of August when Pohangdon and Yonil airbase fell to the NKPA, and an ROK division had to be evacuated by sea to avoid

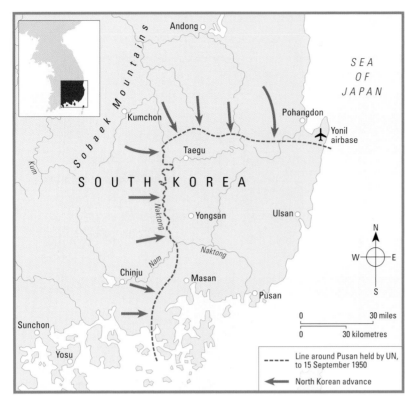

SEA
OF
JAPAN

From end July to mid-September 1950 the NKPA made repeated attacks around the Pusan perimeter. UN forces had fortunately cracked enemy codes and so had warning of each new point of attack.

headquarters for US forces and the seat of the South Korean government. On 18 August the North Koreans came close enough to bring the city under artillery bombardment and the government fled to Pusan. A series of North Korean night attacks in the third week of August, however, failed to break through to Taegu.

KIM IL-SUNG Frustrated at the lack of progress, North Korean leader Kim Il-sung ordered that Pusan was to be captured by 1 September at all costs. But the balance of forces in Korea was shifting in favour of the UN with every week that passed. The North Koreans had suffered heavy losses of both men and equipment. They were now operating far from their home bases, and their long supply lines down the Korean peninsula

destruction. But an ROK counterattack heavily supported by US air strikes and naval bombardments forced the North Koreans back. Then the focus shifted to the area in front of Taegu, which had become the

were under attack from US and Australian aircraft and from UN naval forces patrolling the coast. By contrast, the US ground forces were growing in numbers and improving in quality and equipment. The American

A US tank commander keeps watch from the top of his vehicle outside Taegu in September 1950. Some 4,000 Americans died in the defence of Pusan.

HOLDING THE LINE

On 27 July 1950, General Walton H. Walker, commander of the Eighth US Army in Korea, told his senior officers:

'There will be no more retreating! … We must fight until the end. Capture by these people is worse than death itself … If some of us must die, we will die fighting together … I want everybody to understand that we are going to hold this line. We are going to win …'

[Quoted in *The Korean War*, Brian Catchpole]

and ROK troops were also joined by a British Brigade Group which landed at Pusan at the end of August.

On 31 August General Kim Chaik launched a number of simultaneous offensives around the perimeter. As usual, the North Koreans fought with great determination, but each time they managed a temporary breakthrough Walker's forces proved able to hit back effectively. By 8 September the North Korean offensives had been definitively contained. MacArthur was able to assure the US Joint Chiefs of Staff that the Pusan perimeter would hold.

From the outset of the war, MacArthur had planned a seaborne landing at Inchon. This would enable him to retake Seoul and cut the main communication routes between North Korea and its troops in the South. MacArthur believed that the

North Korean forces could then be crushed and the war brought rapidly to a successful conclusion. Once the Pusan perimeter was reasonably secure the planned amphibious landings – codenamed Operation Chromite – could go ahead.

COMMAND OF THE SEA
The United States and its allies had total command of the seas around Korea. The Americans also had a wealth of experience of amphibious operations accumulated during World War II. But MacArthur's plan nonetheless appeared hazardous. Inchon could only be

US troops land at Inchon in the course of Operation Chromite. The soldiers had to clamber ashore on to sea walls.

CASUALTIES IN OPERATION CHROMITE

The landings at Inchon and the subsequent retaking of Seoul caused the following military casualties:

	Killed/missing in action	Wounded
US Marines	428	2,031
US Army	163	411
US Navy	8	118
ROK Marines/Army	72	198
NKPA (estimate)	14,000	n.a.

approached along a long narrow seaway known as Flying Fish Channel, which was dotted with rocks, reefs and islands, many of which did not appear on naval charts. Landing ships would only be able to come ashore at Inchon at very high tides, which occurred roughly at monthly intervals. As there were no beaches, the landing craft would have to draw up against sea walls near the port.

A new formation was created to run the operation: X Corps, commanded by MacArthur's chief of staff, General Edward Almond. After several days of intensive air and naval bombardment, which devastated the defences around Inchon, the first US Marines landed on the island of Wolmi-do outside Inchon harbour before dawn on 15 September. Further landings followed later in the day, virtually unopposed, and by the morning of 16 September Inchon was in American hands.

Taking Seoul proved a far tougher proposition. Some 20,000 North Korean troops defended the city fearlessly in the face of massive US firepower. The US Marines reached the outskirts of Seoul on 20 September, but the defenders held out for a further eight days, forcing the Americans to fight their way

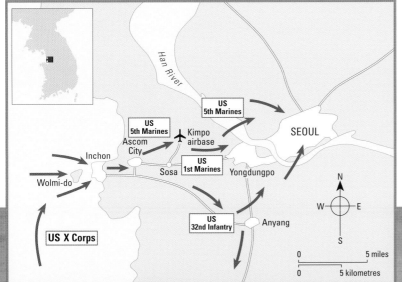

Operation Chromite, launched on 15 September 1950, began with a hazardous amphibious asault on the port of Inchon. Led by US Marines, X Corps then struck inland to seize Seoul.

Landing craft advance towards Inchon. The approaches to the port lay through narrow channels defended by coastal batteries.

American heavy artillery – 155mm howitzers – bombard communist positions in Seoul. The South Korean capital was in ruins by the time UN forces recaptured it in late September 1950.

through the city street by street before it could be secured. By the end of the battle Seoul was an awesome scene of slaughter and destruction.

While the battle for Seoul went on, Walker's Eighth Army went on the attack and broke out of the Pusan perimeter. The breakout had been planned to coincide with the Inchon landings, but North Korean resistance around the perimeter at first remained too strong. On 23 September, however, NKPA troops, fearful of being cut off from the rear by X Corps, began to withdraw northwards. Eighth Army was soon punching holes in the weakening North Korean line. Advanced elements raced north to join up with X Corps near Suwon on 26 September. Three days later MacArthur flew in to Korea in triumph, personally restoring Syngman Rhee to power in Seoul.

MacArthur's sense of triumph was understandable. He had turned the war around,

inflicting heavy losses on the NKPA. As well the large numbers killed, tens of thousands of North Koreans had been taken prisoner. Yet many North Korean units successfully withdrew across the 38th parallel, heading further north to regroup. Many thousands of NKPA soldiers melted away into the South Korean countryside, staying to fight alongside the South Korean guerrillas who had already played a significant part in the conflict.

The fighting had been characterized by massacres and acts of savagery on both sides. The North Koreans frequently shot American soldiers whom they had taken prisoner – usually with a single bullet behind the ear. Both the North and South Koreans were guilty of the mass murder of civilians who had fallen into their hands and whom they decided were political enemies. Nervous American troops, thrown into a desperate battle in a country where many of the peasant

CALL FOR SURRENDER

On 1 October 1950 General MacArthur broadcast a message to the commander of the North Korean forces: *'I, as the United Nations Commander in Chief, call upon you and the forces under your command, in whatever part of Korea situated, forthwith to lay down your arms and cease hostilities under such military supervision as I may direct…'* [Quoted in *The Korean War*, Brian Catchpole]

Retreating North Korean troops were trapped between X Corps, holding Seoul and Suwon, and Eighth Army forces advancing north. Large numbers were captured or killed, but some escaped to join South Korean guerrillas in the mountains.

population supported the communist enemy, often took to firing on civilians on the slightest suspicion that they might be involved in guerrilla activity. Quite apart from such violations of the accepted rules of war, the quantity of firepower deployed by the American forces, especially bombs and napalm dropped from the air, inevitably caused widespread devastation.

The war was now set to move into a new, even more destructive phase. On 27 September MacArthur received permission from the US government to continue the war into the North. He was authorized to advance beyond the 38th parallel to complete the destruction of the enemy army.

A wounded North Korean soldier is held in a prisoner of war (POW) camp in September 1950. POWs on both sides were often grossly mistreated.

CHAPTER 4:
THE CHINESE ENTER THE WAR

American troops advance cautiously near Inchon in 1950. Fighting the Korean War was a particularly grim experience for foot soldiers.

militarily, it would allow MacArthur to complete the destruction of the North Korean army, preventing it from regrouping and rearming for another attack on the South. Politically, it would open the way for the reunification of Korea under an anti-communist government. America's United Nations allies had more serious doubts about the wisdom of carrying the war into the North but felt bound to go along with the United States.

President Truman remained worried about a direct conflict with Communist China or the Soviet Union. MacArthur was authorized to invade North Korea only on condition that Chinese or Soviet forces did not enter the war in support of Kim Il-sung. MacArthur was expressly banned from carrying out military operations, including air strikes, across the Yalu River, which was the border between North Korea and China. He was also ordered to keep US troops at least 65 km away from the Chinese border.

MACARTHUR'S INVASION PLAN

MacArthur's plan for the invasion of North Korea maintained the

The original US and UN military intervention in Korea had been justified as the defence of South Korea against aggression. By the end of September 1950 this act of aggression had been successfully resisted. The continuation of the war with an offensive across the 38th parallel was proposed by MacArthur with enthusiasm, and accepted with some reservations by the US government. They accepted it because,

division between Eighth Army, under General Walker, and X Corps, under General Almond, which had been created for the Inchon landings. Walker's forces were to advance up the west coast, while Almond's were to make a landing at the North Korean port of Wonsan on the east coast.

The movement of X Corps to Wonsan proved a complicated business. It was only possible to move the

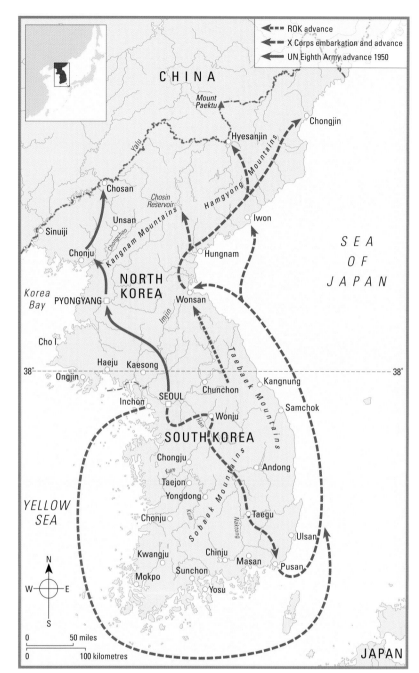

Invading the North, Eighth Army advanced in the west and X Corps with US Marines in the east. ROK units reached the Yalu River at Chosan on 27 October 1950 and X Corps took Hyesanjin on 21 November.

American POWs, taken captive by retreating North Koreans, are paraded in Pyongyang, 1950.

Marines directly by sea from Inchon. The rest of the Corps, some 14,000 men, had to travel across country to Pusan for embarkation. The journey was far from smooth, since guerrillas were operating through much of the area they crossed. By the time X Corps was ready to embark for the planned landings, Wonsan had already been occupied by ROK troops who had advanced overland across the 38th parallel. Since the entrance to Wonsan had been mined, and these mines took time to clear, the Marines were not finally able to land there until 26 October.

By that time the battle for Korea seemed almost over. The Eighth Army had made rapid progress, taking the North Korean capital, Pyongyang, on 12

North Korean civilians inspect their ruined homes after US bombing of Pyongyang in October 1950.

October, and pushing on northward. Syngman Rhee's followers and his police force moved in to Pyongyang and set about establishing his rule there by rounding up and massacring tens of thousands of suspected communists.

MacArthur had originally planned for Eighth Army and X Corps to link up on an east-west line across North Korea roughly at the 40th parallel. But the relative ease of progress made him more confident. He ordered advances northward on both sides of the peninsula, soon authorizing thrusts right up to the Chinese border. By 26 October, advanced units of the ROK 6th Division had reached the Yalu at Chosan. In the east, ROK troops had taken Hungnam and were advancing towards the Chosin Reservoir. At this point, with MacArthur confidently predicting that the Korean War would be over by Christmas, the first reports came in of encounters with Chinese troops.

The Chinese Communist government had begun building up its armed forces along its side of the border with North Korea in July 1950. In early October it gave the United States clear warning that it would take military action if North Korea was invaded. Chinese military commanders were confident that their men could take on and beat the Americans, but China's political leaders were worried about the effect of American airpower. In the second week of October, they obtained from the Soviet Union a promise to supply jet aircraft and to train Chinese pilots to fly them. With this assurance, the order was given for military intervention.

CHINESE PEOPLE'S VOLUNTEERS

Lightly armed troops of the Chinese People's Liberation Army – renamed for service in Korea as the Chinese People's Volunteers (CPV) – began to filter across the Yalu River into North Korea on 19 October. Completely unobserved, they took up positions in the

CHINESE WARNING

On 30 September 1950, Communist Chinese foreign minister Chou En-lai warned the United States in the strongest of terms against invading North Korea, declaring:

'The Chinese people absolutely will not tolerate foreign aggression, nor will they supinely tolerate seeing their neighbours being savagely invaded by imperialists.'
[Quoted in *Rethinking the Korean War*, William Stueck]

Chinese advance to the 38th parallel, December 1950
Area held by UN, end December 1950
Retreat of UN forces to South Korea by sea

Chinese soldiers first crossed the Yalu into Korea in mid-October 1950. They launched a major offensive in late November, driving UN forces back. By Christmas all UN forces had fallen back to the 38th parallel or been evacuated by sea to Pusan.

Chinese soldiers sent to Korea were mostly battle-hardened veterans of the Chinese Civil War.

mountains south of the Yalu, where the remains of the North Korean army were also concealed. On 25 October the Chinese came into contact with UN forces advancing on the Chosin Reservoir in the east and near Unsan in the west (see map, p.25). There were fierce clashes from then until 6 November, with the Eighth Army suffering heavily enough to be forced to pull back and regroup. But the Chinese then withdrew into the mountains again, disappearing as suddenly as they had appeared.

MacArthur recognized the serious implications of Chinese intervention – on 8 November he told the Joint Chiefs of Staff that the movement of Chinese troops across the Yalu 'threatens the ultimate destruction of the forces under my command'. But once his men had lost contact with the Chinese, he chose to assume that the threat was not real. Britain, whose troops were fighting alongside the Americans in North Korea, at this point proposed negotiations with the Chinese, with the aim of establishing a demilitarized zone between the 40th parallel and the Yalu. The suggestion was brushed aside by the United States. On 24 November MacArthur ordered a final drive to the Yalu River that would, he believed, end the war – casually ignoring the instructions he had been given not to send American forces up to the Chinese border.

WINTER WEATHER The UN commanders on the ground were reluctant to take on this ambitious plan. They faced severe

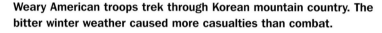

Weary American troops trek through Korean mountain country. The bitter winter weather caused more casualties than combat.

> ## 'AN ENTIRELY NEW WAR…'
>
> On 28 November General MacArthur announced: *'Chinese military forces are committed to North Korea in great and ever increasing strength … We face an entirely new war.'*
> [Quoted in *Rethinking the Korean War,* William Stueck]

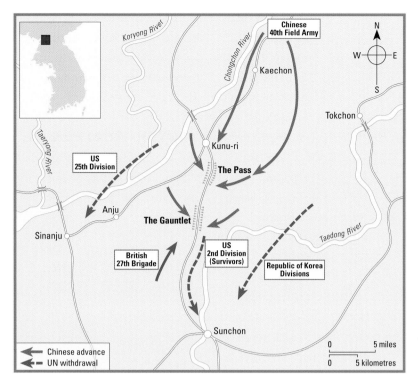

UN forces that had advanced deep into North Korea in November 1950 risked being cut off by fast-moving Chinese infantry operating across country. Ordered to retreat on 28 November, US 2nd Division were ambushed by Chinese forces in passes on the road south to Sunchon and decimated.

winter weather – experienced US Marine commander, General Oliver P. Smith, expressed his belief that 'a winter campaign in the mountains of North Korea is too much to ask of the American soldier or Marine'. They also knew that a Chinese army of unknown strength was somewhere ahead of them. Their worst fears were soon confirmed.

The commander of the Chinese Volunteers, General Peng Dehuai, had at least 200,000 men waiting for this opportunity to launch their own major offensive. Within two days of beginning their advance, the men of Eighth Army – chiefly Americans and South Koreans, with substantial British and Turkish contingents – came

under attack by large numbers of Chinese infantry, aided by North Korean troops and guerrillas. The Chinese operated on foot across country, without artillery, tanks or air support. They tore through the right flank of the Eighth Army, sweeping South Korean forces aside in a few hours. On 28 November Eighth Army was ordered to withdraw, but the Chinese had taken up positions on the road behind them, to the south of the Chongchon River. The retreating UN forces had to fight their way through roadblocks and ambushes, suffering heavy losses of men and equipment. The 2nd Division was so badly hit that it ceased to function as a fighting formation.

In the east, part of X Corps had advanced towards the Yalu across the coastal plain while a smaller force, including US Marines and small number of British Royal Marines, headed across the mountains to the Chosin

US Marines carry a wounded comrade to an airstrip for evacuation to hospital during the fighting in North Korea in the winter of 1950.

Reservoir. Once the scale of the Chinese offensive became apparent, General Almond ordered his forces to withdraw toward the port of Hungnam. The Chosin Reservoir, however, was deep within territory occupied by the Chinese and North Korean guerrillas. The approximately 17,000 UN troops around the reservoir had to fight their way back along narrow roads to the sea. Asked by a journalist whether he would describe this action as a retreat, Marine General Smith replied: 'Retreat, Hell. We're just attacking in a new direction.' The communist forces were unable to prevent the UN troops reaching Hungnam by 11 December.

PYONGYANG WAS ABANDONED

By then the Eighth Army had abandoned North Korea. Once in retreat, it proved impossible to turn the men around to make a stand. By 5 December the UN forces had left the Chinese behind them, but still they continued to head southward, with many American units in complete disarray. Although British troops, were prepared to defend it, Pyongyang was abandoned without a fight. It was what the Americans called 'a bug-out'. Only when they reached the 38th parallel was General Walker able to reform his army and establish a defensive line.

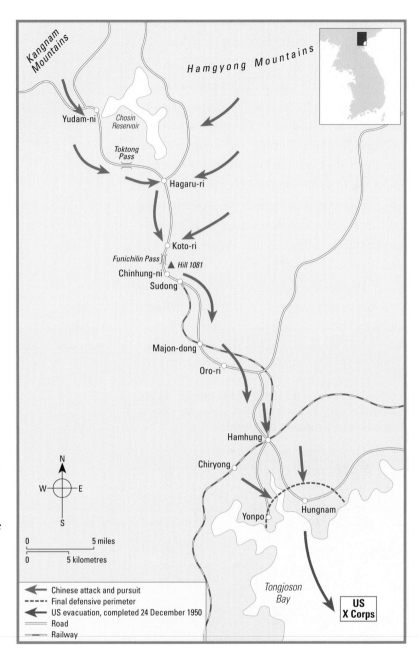

US Marines and other UN troops which had advanced to the Chosin Reservoir were attacked by Chinese forces at the end of November 1950. They held Hagaru-ri in desperate fighting until 6 December. The Marines then fought their way back through the Funichilin Pass and down to the port of Hungnam, which they reached on 11 December.

X Corps moved back to the South in a far more orderly manner, taking ship from Hungnam and other North Korean ports to Pusan. By 24 December, exactly a month after MacArthur had launched his offensive to end the war, no UN forces remained north of the 38th parallel. Kim Il-sung's communists proceeded to reimpose their rule with great brutality.

The UN armies had suffered a humiliating defeat. The Chinese, however, had also taken a severe battering. At least 40,000 men, many of them among their best troops, had been killed. The Soviet Union had fulfilled its promise to send MiG-15 jet fighters with Soviet pilots to bases on the Chinese side of the

North Korean border, and from early November 1950 they engaged in battles with American aircraft near the Yalu River. But the MiGs did not venture further south and US aircraft remained unchallenged over most of Korea. Using bombs, rockets and napalm, they imposed heavy casualties on Chinese troops. Also, although the Chinese infantry on the whole coped better with the harsh conditions than their enemies, thousands of soldiers suffered from exposure to the extreme cold, contracting frostbite or even in some cases freezing to death. Many units ran desperately short of food – unless they could capture some of the Americans' lavish supplies.

By the end of December 1950, the Chinese and their North Korean allies were sufficiently reorganized and resupplied to resume their offensive, striking across the 38th parallel. After six months of bitter fighting, the ground war was back where it had started.

Turkish troops serving with the UN forces prepare to fight a delaying action against the advancing Chinese in December 1950.

US soldiers take a rest behind the lines in South Korea, January 1951. Even away from the enemy, there was no escaping the weather.

CASUALTIES OF COLD

Among US Marines retreating from the Chosin Reservoir, the extreme cold put more men out of action than the fighting. Marine casualties November-December 1950 were:

Killed in action	718
Missing	192
Wounded in action	3,508
Non-battle casualties	7,313

The Chinese entry into the war in Korea created an acute sense of crisis in the United States in the winter of 1950-1. There was a real fear that the Korean War might be about to lead to a worldwide 'total war' between the United States and its allies on one side and the Soviet Union and its allies – including Communist China – on the other. President Truman expressed this fear on 9 December 1950, writing: 'It looks like World War III is here...' It was expected that if a world war did occur, nuclear weapons would be used by the United States and also probably by the Soviet Union – the Soviets had exploded their first atom bomb in a test in 1949.

THE THREAT OF A WORLD WAR

The threat of a world war, which both the United States and the Soviet Union wanted to avoid, meant that both sides followed self-imposed rules designed to prevent the Korean War escalating. For example, although

President Truman and Prime Minister Attlee (foreground left and right) meet in December 1950. Attlee opposed the use of atom bombs in Korea.

The UN General Assembly – seen here in 1949 – maintained majority support for American policy in Korea throughout the war.

Soviet pilots took part in the air war fought over North Korea, clashing directly with US pilots, the Soviet Union always denied that its aircrew were in the country and limited their operations – they never flew over areas occupied by UN troops. US aircraft did not attack targets inside China, including communist air bases.

Faced with the desperate military situation in Korea at the end of 1950, however, the American government was tempted to break the self-imposed limits set on military action. Two major options were considered. One was to widen the war by attacking the Chinese mainland from the air and sea to destroy China's capacity to wage war. The other was to escalate the war by using atom bombs. Both these options were urged by General MacArthur and strongly opposed by America's major UN allies, including Britain.

At the end of November 1950 a crisis occurred in America's relations with its allies when President Truman hinted publicly that the use of atom bombs in Korea was not ruled out. The leader of the British Labour government, Prime Minister Clement Attlee, had faithfully supported the Americans over Korea, politically and

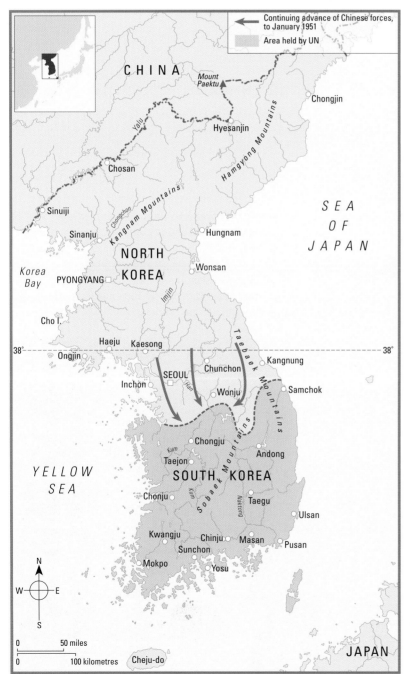

Continuing advance of Chinese forces, to January 1951

Area held by UN

NATIONAL EMERGENCY

On 16 December 1950 US President Truman declared a national state of emergency, telling the American people: *'Our homes, our nation, all the things we believe in are in great danger … I summon our farmers, our workers in industry and our businessmen to make a mighty production effort to meet the defense requirements of the nation…'* [Quoted in *Korea: The Unknown War*, Jon Halliday and Bruce Cumings]

The communist forces launched a fresh offensive at New Year 1951, soon recaptured Seoul, and advanced about 80 km south of the city. There UN forces at last formed a defensive line that held its ground.

militarily, despite outspoken criticism of the war by some Labour members of parliament (MPs). The suggestion that the United States might use atom bombs caused uproar in the House of Commons and Attlee asked for an urgent meeting with Truman. In talks in Washington in early December, Attlee extracted from Truman a promise that atom bombs would not be used without Britain first being consulted.

CHINA'S LEGITIMATE GOVERNMENT

The United States never, however, finally ruled out the use of atom bombs in Korea and US leaders continued to discuss them as a military option up to the end of the war. Britain also failed to persuade the United States to take a less hostile line on Communist China. The United

Chinese Volunteers who have been taken prisoner are guarded by US Marines in January 1951 – a rare local success for the UN forces at this desperate stage of the war.

From January to April 1951, under the command of General Ridgway, UN forces steadily pushed the communists back in a series of offensives marked by the heavy use of artillery and air strikes.

States had committed itself to the support of Chiang Kai-shek's Chinese Nationalists based on Formosa (Taiwan) and would not recognize the communists as China's legitimate government. After a British-sponsored UN peace initiative was rejected by China in January 1951, Britain reluctantly supported the United States in having Communist China condemned by the UN as an 'aggressor state'.

Fortunately, a change in the military situation in Korea in the first half of 1951 dampened down the acute crisis. The year started with a renewed communist offensive that once more sent the UN forces reeling into retreat. Chinese troops attacked across the frozen Imjin River before dawn on New Year's Day. Blowing bugles and shouting insults they

DISORDERLY RETREAT

General Matthew B. Ridgway, commander of Eighth Army, described the unruly retreat of South Korean troops in the face of the first Chinese offensive of 1951:

'On New Year's morning I drove out north of Seoul and into a dismaying spectacle. ROK soldiers by truckloads were streaming south, without order, without arms, without leaders, in full retreat. Some came on foot, or in commandeered vehicles of every sort. They had just one aim – to get as far away from the Chinese as possible.'

[Quoted in *The War in Korea*, Matthew B. Ridgway]

with fresh troops and equipment. Ridgway had to find a way to make his increased strength effective on the battlefield. The lightly armed Chinese had achieved their successes largely through mobility and surprise, infiltrating and overrunning UN positions in a way that unnerved and demoralized UN troops. Ridgway set out to establish an unbroken line from coast to coast across the peninsula, so that his men could not be outflanked or surrounded. This line was to advance up the peninsula, preceded by an intensive barrage of artillery fire and air attacks which would destroy the enemy without the need for costly assaults by UN infantry. This tactic was chillingly dubbed the 'meatgrinder'.

COUNTER-OFFENSIVE

Ridgway launched his counter-offensive on 25 January 1951. The new tactics proved very effective. On the western flank, by 10 February UN forces had recaptured Inchon and

bore down upon the South Korean troops on the other bank, most of whom simply turned and fled. The Eighth Army was now under a new commander, General Matthew B. Ridgway, after the death of General Walker in a road accident. Ridgway witnessed with dismay the flight of his troops from the battlefield. The failure of so many of his soldiers to stand and fight left him with no choice but to order a general withdrawal. The decision to abandon Seoul was taken on 3 January. Over the following week UN forces fell back some 70 or 80 km south of the city. American leaders discussed a possible evacuation of all UN ground troops from Korea.

But, reliant on supplies carried mostly on the backs of human porters down the length of the Korean peninsula, the Chinese army was running out of ammunition and food. The Chinese and North Koreans had also suffered heavy casualties and replacement troops were slow to arrive. By mid-January their offensive had run out of steam and they came to a halt. This respite gave Ridgway the chance to organize the first effective UN counter-offensive since the Chinese entered the war.

The UN forces were being rapidly strengthened

General Matthew B. Ridgway (right) restored the morale of US troops and initiated a war of attrition – the 'meatgrinder' tactics.

Weapons using burning petrol – such as this flamethrower and napalm bombs – were widely employed in Korea. They caused horrific injuries.

reached the Han River. In one five-day period 4,200 Chinese soldiers were reckoned to have been killed for the loss of only 70 UN troops. The Chinese responded by attempting to overcome their enemy's firepower with sheer numbers. They adopted 'human wave' tactics in which thousands of infantry rushed forward in mass frontal attacks on UN positions. These tactics achieved some successes, but at enormous human cost.

Ridgway's offensive ground forward through February and March in a series of operations codenamed, with deliberate ruthlessness, Thunderbolt, Killer, and Ripper. Seoul, by this time the devastated shell of a city, was retaken on 14 March. By 21 April UN forces in the centre and east had once more edged north of the 38th parallel, with the front line in the west running along the Imjin River.

With South Korea back in UN hands, President Truman began to prepare a peace initiative, a course strongly urged by his UN allies. General MacArthur, however, remained totally opposed to the idea of compromise with the Chinese Communists. MacArthur saw the objective of the war as total military victory and was not ready to stop short of controlling Korea up to the Yalu River. He not only argued for strikes against targets inside mainland China, but also wanted Chiang Kai-shek's Chinese Nationalist troops brought in to the war against the Communist Chinese.

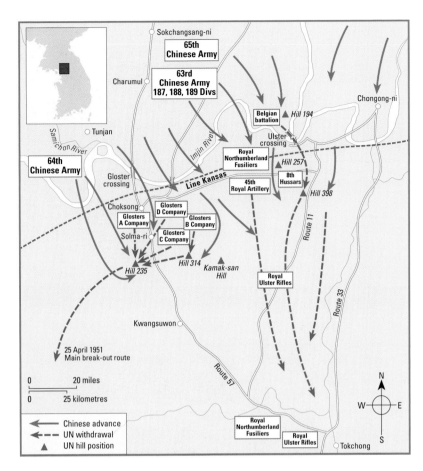

On 22 April 1951 Chinese troops crossed the Imjin River on a sector of the front held by British forces. Surrounded by the enemy, four companies of the Gloucestershire Regiment (the Glosters) held crucial hill positions for three days. Only 39 men eventually escaped.

MACARTHUR'S POLICY

General MacArthur's dismissal followed his public threat, on 24 March 1951, to extend the war to a direct attack on China:

'The enemy [China] *must by now be painfully aware that a decision of the United Nations to depart from its tolerant effort to confine the war to the area of Korea, through an expansion of our military operations to his coastal areas and interior bases, would doom Red China to the risk of imminent military collapse.'*

[Quoted in *The War in Korea*, Matthew B. Ridgway]

MACARTHUR IS DISMISSED

America's UN allies had come to distrust MacArthur deeply – British Foreign Secretary Herbert Morrison described him as 'rash and politically irresponsible'. The American government feared that MacArthur might widen the war by some military action ordered on his own authority. After the general pressed publicly for a more aggressive policy, in direct defiance of instructions from his government, Truman dismissed him from all his commands on 11 April. MacArthur was a powerful and popular figure in the United States, and his dismissal caused a political storm. General Ridgway was promoted to replace MacArthur as UN Commander, while General James Van Fleet took over from Ridgway as army commander on the ground in Korea.

General Van Fleet was faced almost immediately by a fresh military crisis. Despite the heavy losses that they had sustained over the previous months of intense fighting, on 22 April the Chinese once more took the offensive. This time, however, the UN forces were better organized and equipped for defence, and in most instances were prepared to stand and fight – to the death if necessary.

This was nowhere more notable than on the sector of the Imjin River held by the British 29th Brigade. Despite the Brigade's valiant efforts, the Chinese broke through their line. The four companies of the Gloucestershire Regiment ('Glosters') fighting with the 29th Brigade were encircled by the enemy, but still held out for three days. In the end, all but 39 of the Glosters were killed or taken prisoner.

Still regarded as a national hero, General MacArthur is given a tickertape welcome on Broadway, New York, after being sacked as commander of the UN forces in Korea by President Truman in April 1951.

CHINA'S OFFENSIVE IS REPULSED

In the face of such determined resistance, the communist offensive came to a halt at the end of April just short of Seoul. The Chinese and North Koreans are reckoned to have lost some 70,000 men in nine days' fighting, compared with UN losses of about 7,000. A renewed Chinese effort in mid-May achieved little and the exhausted communist forces were soon once more withdrawing northward to the 38th parallel and beyond.

By June 1951, another half year of desperately destructive warfare had again brought the two sides more or less back where the war had started.

RISING NUMBERS

By May 1951, the United States estimated the numbers of troops involved in the fighting as follows:

Chinese	542,000
North Korean	197,000
Total communist	**739,000**
US and UN allies	270,000
South Korean	240,000
Total UN	**510,000**

The Chinese launched an offensive on 22 April that pushed south through the following week. But stiff UN resistance from 1-15 May checked the Chinese advance short of the city of Seoul. A second Chinese effort from 16 May soon ran out of steam, and their forces soon began to withdraw northwards across the 38th parallel.

US Marines watch rocket artillery fire as Chinese positions are heavily bombarded. From 1951 onwards, the war was increasingly a contest of UN firepower pitted against Chinese numbers.

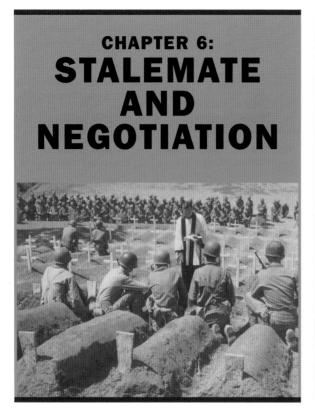

A funeral service is held for US soldiers killed in action. The heavy loss of American lives influenced the US government to seek a ceasefire.

US Marines search a Chinese soldier they have captured. Chinese losses in the fighting – killed and captured – were on a massive scale.

In June 1951 the Chinese Communist government told the Soviet Union that it intended to seek an armistice in Korea. In the same month, the United States privately indicated to the Soviet Ambassador to the UN, Jacob Malik, that a ceasefire at or around the 38th parallel would be acceptable to the United States. With both sides apparently prepared to end the fighting, prospects for rapid agreement looked good. Yet the ceasefire negotiations, which began in July 1951, in fact went on for two years – a period during which many hundreds of thousands of lives were lost.

THE 38TH PARALLEL The failure to make progress in the talks was especially frustrating because the two sides were in rough agreement on the main issue from the outset. They accepted that a ceasefire would, at least for the time being, leave Korea divided at or around the 38th parallel as it had been before the war started. Both Chinese and US leaders had come to the conclusion that the cost of attempting to win the war was too high for any advantage they might stand to gain from a united Korea.

From the summer of 1951 onward, the purpose of the fighting on both sides was not to achieve military victory but to keep up pressure on the enemy while negotiations took place. The UN forces made a last substantial advance in August-October 1951, though

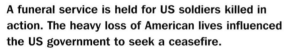

OPPOSING ARMIES

Estimated troops levels of the two armies confronting one another in Korea in the last years of the war were:

	Dec 1951	Dec 1952	July 1953
UN forces	600,000	768,000	932,000
Communist forces	800,000	900,000	1,200,000

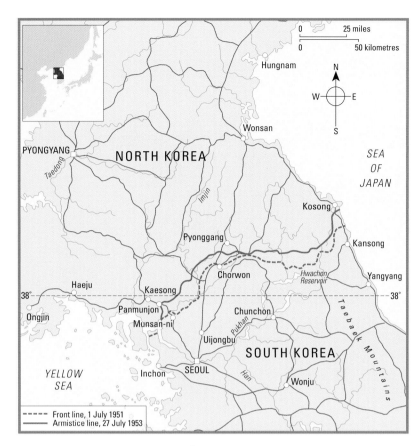

Front line, 1 July 1951
Armistice line, 27 July 1953

they could only push the front line northward by dint of extremely heavy fighting and a corresponding high level of casualties. From November 1951 both sides dug in to what the UN forces called the Main Line of Resistance, entrenched positions across the peninsula where they would remain for the rest of the war.

While the outside powers no longer sought to unify Korea by military victory, their Korean allies, North and South, were far from

The last two years of the war – the time it took to negotiate a ceasefire – saw stalemate on the battlefield. The line finally agreed to separate North and South Korea was not very different from the front line when talks began.

The battleship USS *Missouri* bombards the North Korean coast in May 1951. Shelling by UN warships devastated virtually all of North Korea's port cities, coastal roads and railways.

The UN delegates at the ceasefire talks pose for the cameras in Kaesong, August 1951. Vice-Admiral Turner Joy, the head of the delegation, stands in the middle of the group.

happy with this shift of position. In the North, Kim Il-sung reluctantly accepted that reunification was not on the agenda – he was in a weak position, with his own North Korean forces reduced to a relatively small military role alongside the Chinese and his country under constant attack by American aircraft and warships. In the South, Syngman Rhee was less docile. He protested fiercely against a ceasefire that would leave the communists in control of the North and tried to drum up support in the US Congress for continuing the war until the North was conquered. Rhee had no real influence on the US government, however. The ROK was given only token representation at the ceasefire negotiations, which were conducted by the Americans on one side and the North Koreans and Chinese on the other.

The two sides agreed to open negotiations on 10 July 1951 at Kaesong, in the no man's land between the two armies. Before the talks started, however, communist forces seized the Kaesong area. The head of

the UN delegation, Vice-Admiral Turner Joy, thus found himself on the first day of talks meeting the communist negotiators in a building surrounded by North Korean troops. It was eventually agreed to make Kaesong a neutral zone free of military personnel, but the negotiations had got off to a bad start.

LACK OF TRUST   There was a total lack of trust and mutual respect between the two sides. General Ridgway referred to the communists as 'treacherous savages' who could not be talked to in the same way as 'enlightened and civilized people'. The chief North Korean negotiator, Nam Il, accused the American representatives of not coming to make peace but 'to look for an excuse for extending the war'. In August the communists accused the UN of an air attack on the conference zone and talks were suspended for over a month before resuming in tents at nearby Panmunjon in October.

At the end of November 1951 the two sides

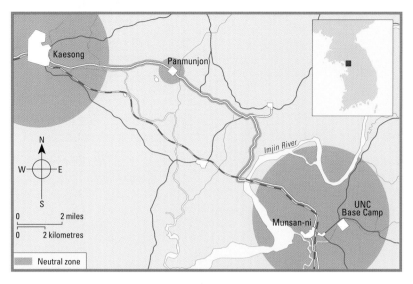

The armistice talks began at Kaesong on the Chinese side of the front line, but from October 1951 the talks shifted to Panmunjon. The area of the talks was declared a neutral zone between the conflicting armies.

tentatively agreed on an armistice line – basically the 'line of contact' between the positions that the two armies had reached at that point in the fighting. The following February there was broad agreement on how a ceasefire would be carried out and supervised. The only major issue then outstanding was the exchange of prisoners of war (POWs). This turned into an absolute block to further progress. There were some 150,000 POWs held by the UN and a substantial but considerably smaller number held in North Korea. The procedure laid down in the Geneva Convention, widely accepted as setting rules for the conduct of war, was for both sides to hand over all their POWs at the end of a conflict. The Americans, however, did not accept an 'all-for-all' exchange. They argued that POWs must have a free choice of whether or not to return to communist North Korea or China. This predictably outraged the communist negotiators.

Attempts to find out whether POWs really wanted to be returned or not were rendered impossible in

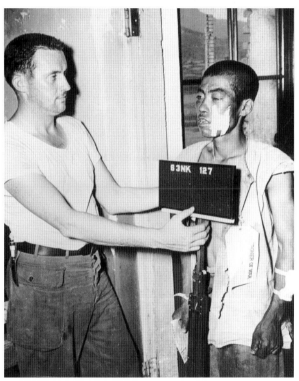

A communist POW has an identification photo taken at a prison camp. The details of exchanging POWs were a stumbling block in the ceasefire talks.

CHINESE PROPAGANDA

The Chinese tried to undermine the morale of UN troops on the Main Line of Resistance with propaganda – for example, distributing Christmas cards with the following message:

'*Dear Soldiers, It is Christmas and you are far from home not knowing when you will die. The big shots are home, enjoying themselves, eating good food, drinking good liquor. Why should you be here risking your life for their profits ?...A Merry Christmas and a Happy New Year, From the Chinese People's Volunteers.*'

[Quoted in *The Korean War*, Brian Catchpole]

UN forces occupied North Korean coastal islands, from where they raided the mainland. The bombing of dams deprived North Korea of power and ruined irrigation systems. MiG jet bases on the Chinese side of the border were off limits for US bombers.

practice by the brutal and chaotic conditions in POW camps in South Korea. Prisoners were subjected to intimidation both by fellow prisoners and by camp authorities. An uprising by prisoners at the Koje camp in May 1952 had to be crushed by UN military forces with the use of tanks. Meanwhile the treatment of POWs in North Korea also became a subject of concern, with allegations of ill-treatment and 'brainwashing' – psychological pressure and indoctrination – designed to make the UN prisoners convert to communism or denounce the actions of their own side.

As the negotiations dragged on, so did the war. In the winter of 1951-2, much of the UN fighting effort went into establishing full

US Air Force B-29 Superfortresses bomb targets in North Korea. Almost every town and city in the North was devastated by bombing.

In March 1951 Admiral Allan F. Smith described the effect of UN naval bombardment on the North Korean port city of Wonsan: '*In Wonsan you cannot walk in the streets. You cannot sleep anywhere in the 24 hours, unless it is the sleep of death.*'

[Quoted in *Korea: The Unknown War*, Jon Halliday and Bruce Cumings]

A US Navy F-4U Corsair takes off from an aircraft carrier for a ground attack mission against communist forces.

control of South Korea. Many areas, especially in the south-west, were still dominated by South Korean left-wing guerrillas and by North Korean soldiers who had been left behind when their original invasion of the South was defeated. ROK General Paek Sun-yop claimed to have largely destroyed the guerrilla movement by the end of January 1952 in an operation codenamed 'Ratkiller'.

NAVAL AND AIR ATTACKS
Naval and air attacks on North Korea were the most important way that the UN forces kept up pressure on the communist side during the stalled negotiations. With

uncontested control of the sea, the warships of the United States and its allies were able to lay waste North Korean coastal towns with uninterrupted bombardment by their powerful guns. UN forces were also able to seize islands close to the North Korean coast and use them as bases from which to send small groups of special forces across to the mainland on intelligence-gathering and sabotage missions.

Aircraft carriers contributed to the large-scale bombardment of North Korea from the air, which was also carried out by aircraft based in Japan and South Korea. One aim of the air attacks was to cut supply routes from China and the Soviet Union to the communist army in the front line. But bombing was also used as a means of inflicting punishment on the North Koreans, in the hope that this would undermine popular support for Kim Il-sung or persuade the communists to give way in the ceasefire negotiations. Pyongyang and virtually every other town or city of any size in North Korea was devastated by air attacks. On 23 June 1952, in a deliberate escalation of the air war, the huge Supung dam on the Yalu River was

American artillerymen cover their ears as a heavy gun is fired at night, October 1952. Communist troops sheltered deep inside tunnels to find protection against shelling.

destroyed by bombing, along with three other dams, depriving all of North Korea and much of north-east China of their electricity supply.

Meanwhile the ground war on the Main Line of Resistance remained a very costly stalemate. To protect themselves from UN air attacks and artillery, the Chinese and North Koreans dug a network of tunnels about 1,200 km long. In this underground fortress they built up their forces until, by early 1953, there were reckoned to be a million Chinese soldiers committed to the war. They were faced by around 800,000 UN troops. Although neither side was even seeking a military victory, the local and limited offensives they launched, especially in the autumn of 1952, were fiercely fought and left many thousands dead.

CLARK TAKES CHARGE There were changes of leadership on the American side, with General Mark Clark taking over as UN Commander from General Ridgway in May 1952, and Dwight D. Eisenhower, a famous US World War II general, replacing Truman as US president in January 1953. But the crucial change came in the communist camp, when Soviet dictator Joseph Stalin died on 5 March 1953. The new Soviet leadership soon indicated that it saw no reason why an agreement on a ceasefire should be any longer delayed. The talks resumed with a new sense of purpose.

With an armistice agreement at last almost within reach, both sides stepped up the military pressure. In May 1953 the UN air force bombed irrigation dams

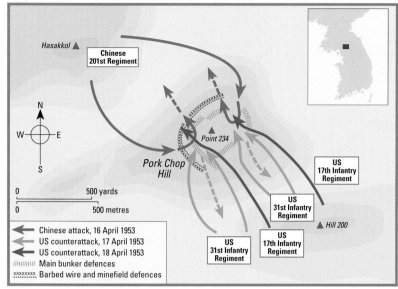

Hasakkol ▲

Chinese
201st Regiment

N
W—E
S

Point 234

Pork Chop
Hill

US
17th Infantry
Regiment

US
31st Infantry
Regiment

▲ Hill 200

US
31st Infantry
Regiment

US
17th Infantry
Regiment

0   500 yards
0   500 metres

← Chinese attack, 16 April 1953
← US counterattack, 17 April 1953
← US counterattack, 18 April 1953
||||||||| Main bunker defences
xxxxxxxx Barbed wire and minefield defences

On the static front line, insignificant features were fought over with great ferocity. In April 1953 one such position, Pork Chop Hill, changed hands twice in three days – first seized by the Chinese, then retaken by the Americans.

north of Pyongyang creating widespread flooding and destroying the North Korean rice crop, so the entire population was threatened with starvation. Eisenhower hinted that atom bombs might be used if a ceasefire was not soon agreed. The Chinese maximized pressure along the front line on the ground. Between April and July 1953 large forces fought bitter battles for outposts of no special significance. One such position, Pork Chop Hill, became of such symbolic importance that by July the Americans had five battalions deployed on a hill that had once been defended by 100 men, while the Chinese were prepared to attack it with an entire division. In a single week in July 1953 UN casualties at the front numbered almost 30,000, and casualties on the communist side were probably more than double that figure.

Syngman Rhee made a last desperate attempt to sabotage the ceasefire talks in June by releasing POWs, so they could not be returned to the North. But an agreement on the POW issue was nonetheless hammered out. On 27 July 1953 an armistice was signed at Panmunjon by General William K. Harrison for the UN command and by Nam Il for the communist forces. Three years and 33 days after it had begun, the war was over.

On 27 July 1953 the commander of UN forces, General Mark Clark, signs the armistice agreement at his headquarters, after the initial signing at Panmunjon.

CHAPTER 7:
CONSEQUENCES OF THE WAR

The foreign ministers of the United States, Britain, France, the Soviet Union and Communist China met at Geneva in April 1954 to discuss the future of Korea and Indo-China. No agreement was reached on Korea.

Under the terms of the armistice, an international conference was to be held to negotiate a final peace agreement. The Geneva Conference duly assembled in April 1954, but no progress was made on Korea. The UN side proposed reunification after nationwide elections under UN supervision. The communists countered by demanding the withdrawal of all foreign forces from Korea before elections could be held. Negotiations went no further. The United States had already signed a Mutual Defense Treaty with South Korea in August 1953, committing its forces to the defence of the South – they were

still there 50 years later. Korea was left divided by a demilitarized zone along the ceasefire line.

The war had important effects outside Korea. In Asia, it led directly to the economic and political recovery of Japan after the devastation of World War II. Japanese industry expanded rapidly through supplying the needs of the UN war machine. Politically, Japan was transformed from America's most hated enemy of World War II into a valued ally. The war also confirmed the alliance between the United States and the Chinese Nationalists on Taiwan. America's relations with Communist China remained totally hostile until the 1970s – the government in Beijing was finally allowed to represent China at the UN in 1971.

Inevitably, a war that cost almost 34,000 American lives had a considerable impact on the United States. It brought anti-communist sentiment to its highest pitch – between 1950 and 1954, Senator Joe McCarthy was the most prominent figure engaged in a 'witchhunt' that sought to root out communist sympathisers in all areas of American life. Yet for the 1.8 million Americans who had served in Korea it soon came to seem the 'Forgotten War' – there was no memorial to the Korean War veterans in Washington D.C. until 1995.

US political and military leaders were keen to avoid any repetition of the heavy casualties in Korea. The Eisenhower

SCENE OF DEVASTATION

Devastated by bombing, the condition of North Korean cities at the end of the war was witnessed by Hungarian author Tibor Meray. He said: *'I don't know why houses collapsed and chimneys did not, but I went through a city of 200,000 inhabitants and I saw thousands of chimneys – and that was all.'*

[Quoted in *The Guardian* newspaper, 11 April 2000]

administration regarded having got involved in a 'limited war' as a serious mistake. If such an act of 'communist aggression' occurred again, they planned to respond immediately by using nuclear weapons. But in the 1960s the United States found itself fighting another war on the ground in Asia, in Vietnam, with a similar policy of keeping the war 'limited' – and similar heavy casualties.

For Koreans on both sides of the ceasefire line, the war had been a catastrophe. Probably around one in ten of the Korean population were killed. Most towns and cities were heaps of ruins. Factories, roads, railways and dams were destroyed. The economic hardship experienced in the wake of this destruction was made worse by political oppression. There was no democracy or freedom in the North or the South. Kim Il-sung built North Korea into a regimented single-party

The result of the Korean War, in which millions died, was a minor adjustment of the border between North and South. Fifty years later, the two countries were still divided along the armistice line.

American forces in Vietnam in 1969: the Vietnam War had obvious similarities to the Korean conflict, with a communist North and a pro-American South.

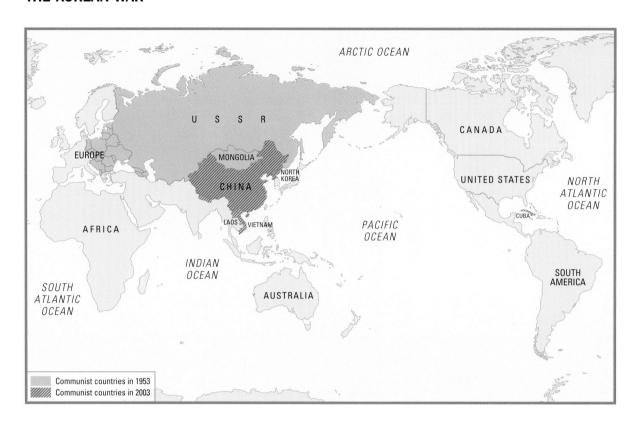

Communist countries in 1953
Communist countries in 2003

communist dictatorship which he ruled as the 'Great Leader'. In South Korea, Syngman Rhee ruled as the authoritarian dictator of a police state.

Over time, conditions north and south of the ceasefire line diverged. In the South, Rhee was forced to resign after a student uprising in 1960. There followed a long period of military-dominated government, with opposition politicians frequently arrested or in other ways harassed or suppressed. Genuine multi-party democracy did finally arrive in South Korea, however, in 1988. By then, the South Korean economy had been transformed through state-sponsored capitalism, which produced spectacular growth in shipbuilding, car-making, and other manufacture for export. Most of the population shared in the

In 1953 North Korea was part of a powerful bloc of communist-ruled states stretching from the Pacific to central Europe. By 2004, the communist world had shrunk significantly.

The authoritarian South Korean President Syngman Rhee (left) meets South Vietnamese leader Ngo Dinh Diem in 1958. Two years later Rhee was forced to resign, but democracy was slow to follow.

prosperity this industrial expansion generated, enjoying fast-improving living conditions.

There were no such developments in North Korea. Kim Il-sung ruled until his death in 1994, when he was succeeded by his son, Kim Jong-il. After the collapse of communism in Eastern Europe and the Soviet Union in 1989-91 and the adoption of free-market economic policies by Communist China from the 1980s, North Korea was left as the world's most hardline communist state. The vast majority of its population lived in poverty – in the 1990s there were reports of widespread starvation – and had no personal freedom or human rights.

Over the years relations between North and South have generally been hostile, with occasional minor military clashes or incidents either at sea or across the demilitarized zone. From the 1990s there have been some attempts to create closer relations, with a view to eventual reunification – most notably an official visit by South Korean president Kim Dae-jung to the North in 2000 – but with limited effect.

Fifty years after the end of the Korean War, relations between the United States and North Korea were still antagonistic. In 2002 US President George W.

A veteran of the Korean War salutes as he visits the Korean War Veterans Memorial in Washington D.C. Part of the memorial consists of 19 statues created by sculptor Frank Gaylord that represent an American military unit on patrol in Korea.

Bush put North Korea on his list of 'rogue states' because of its alleged development of nuclear weapons. There was still a long journey to make before the legacy of the war could finally be overcome.

BUSH CONFRONTS NORTH KOREA

In October 2003, on a visit to Thailand, President George W. Bush told journalists: *'I've said as plainly as I can that we have no intention of invading North Korea [but] we expect North Korea to get rid of her nuclear ambitions. … She must get rid of her weapons programs …'* [Office of the Press Secretary, The White House, 19 October 2003]

GENERAL EDWARD ALMOND (1892-1979)

Born in Virginia, Almond was chief of staff to General MacArthur when the Korean War broke out in June 1950. In September MacArthur gave Almond command of X Corps, which was entrusted with the Inchon landings. He remained X Corps commander for the invasion of North Korea and through the subsequent evacuation of the North. Almond left Korea in July 1951, retiring from the Army two years later.

CLEMENT ATTLEE (1883-1967)

British politician Clement Attlee was first elected to parliament as a Labour MP in 1922. He became leader of the Labour Party in 1935 and was a member of Winston Churchill's coalition government during World War II. After Labour's landslide victory in the 1945 general election he became prime minister, a post he held until 1951. Attlee loyally supported the United States in the Korean War, overriding opposition from many Labour MPs. He tried to be a moderating influence on US policy.

CHIANG KAI-SHEK (1887-1975)

Chinese general Chiang Kai-shek became head of the Chinese Nationalist government in 1928. He fought to suppress the Chinese Communists, led by Mao Tse-tung, and from 1937 was also engaged in a war with Japan. An ally of Britain and the United States during World War II, he received large amounts of US aid, but was nonetheless defeated by the Communists in the Chinese Civil War of 1945-9. Chiang and his supporters took refuge on Formosa (Taiwan). His offer of Chinese Nationalist troops to take part in the Korean War was refused by the United States, although General MacArthur had wanted to accept. The confrontation with Communist China brought about by the war ensured that the United States would continue to back his Nationalist government. Chiang still claimed to be the rightful ruler of China at his death in 1975.

GENERAL MARK W. CLARK (1896-1984)

Born in New York, General Clark made his name during World War II first in the fighting in North Africa from 1942 to 1943, and then as Allied commander in Italy. In May 1952 he took over from General Ridgway as UN Commander in Korea. In this capacity he signed the armistice in July 1953, continuing as head of the UN forces until the following October.

DWIGHT D. EISENHOWER (1890-1969)

Born in Texas, Eisenhower rose to fame as a general in World War II. He was supreme commander of Allied forces for the D-Day landings in 1944 and for the subsequent campaign in Europe. When NATO (the North Atlantic Treaty Organization) was formed in 1949, Eisenhower was its first military commander. In 1952 he moved into politics and, as the Republican candidate, won US presidential elections. Expectations that he might take a tougher line on Korea, and even authorize the use of nuclear weapons, helped push the Chinese toward accepting a negotiated settlement in 1953. Eisenhower remained president until 1961.

KIM IL-SUNG (1912-94)

Born when Korea was already under the control of Japan, as a young man Kim Il-sung joined guerrillas fighting against the Japanese in Manchuria. He returned to the Soviet-occupied zone of Korea after the Japanese surrender in 1945 and became leader of the communist Korean Workers' Party. With Soviet backing, he founded the Korean People's Democratic Republic in 1948. He launched the invasion of South Korea in June 1950 in the hope of uniting the country under communist rule. Despite the failure to achieve unification, he remained ruler of North Korea for the rest of his life. He combined hardline communism with a personal dictatorship – he was known as the 'Great Leader' and, when he died, passed on control of North Korea to his son.

ADMIRAL C. TURNER JOY (1895-1956)

Born in Missouri, Charles Turner Joy was commander of US Naval Forces, Far East, when the Korean War broke out in June 1950. He performed ably in establishing total supremacy at sea and deploying his warships in support of land operations. In July 1951 he was chosen to head the UN delegation to the armistice talks. He found the negotiations a frustrating experience and was reassigned at his own request in April 1952.

GENERAL DOUGLAS MACARTHUR (1880-1964)

Born into a military family in Arkansas, MacArthur fought with distinction in World War I. During World War II he was America's senior army commander in the Pacific. By the time Japan surrendered in 1945, MacArthur was a national hero. He effectively ruled Japan during the period of military occupation that followed. Given command of UN forces in Korea in 1950, he was responsible for the landings at Inchon which turned the tide of the war. Overconfidence, however, blinded him to the threat of Chinese intervention after his forces entered North Korea. The military disaster of November-December 1950 weakened his authority. MacArthur was increasingly open in his criticism of the policies of President Truman, advocating direct attacks on Communist China, the use of Chinese nationalist troops, and the use of atom bombs. Truman dismissed him in April 1951.

MAO TSE-TUNG
(1893-1976)

A founder member of the Chinese Communist Party in 1921, Mao emerged as the movement's undisputed leader in the 1930s. Developing support among the peasant population of rural China, he fought a guerrilla war against Chiang Kai-shek's Nationalists and, between 1937 and 1945, against the Japanese. He proclaimed the communist People's Republic of China in Beijing in 1949. His decision to send troops into the Korean War enabled North Korea to survive, but at great cost in lives – one of those who died was his own son. Mao remained China's leader until his death.

PAEK SUN-YOP (1921-)

South Korean army officer Paek Sun-yop was a colonel in command of the ROK 1st Infantry Division when the North Koreans invaded in June 1950. He was soon marked out as the most effective of ROK officers, performing well during the defence of the Pusan perimeter. He took part in the ill-fated invasion of the North in October-December 1950 and, in the winter of 1951-2, was in charge of anti-guerrilla operations in South Korea (Operation Ratkiller). He was made ROK army chief of staff in 1952.

GENERAL PENG DEHUAI
(1898-1974)

Peng Dehuai was one of Mao Tse-tung's companions on the famous Long March of 1934, in which the Chinese Communists escaped destruction by Chiang Kai-shek's Nationalists. He was a prominent military commander in the guerrilla war against the Japanese in China from 1937 and in the Chinese Civil War, which brought the communists to power in Beijing in 1949. Peng commanded the Chinese Volunteers throughout the Korean War. After the war he was Chinese minister of defence, but in 1959 he expressed criticisms of Mao's policies that put him out of favour. In 1966, during the upheaval known as the Cultural Revolution, he was arrested and tortured. He was still under house arrest at the time of his death.

GENERAL MATTHEW B. RIDGWAY (1895-1993)

Born in Virginia, Ridgway commanded airborne forces in Europe during World War II. Appointed commander of Eighth Army on General Walker's death in December 1950, he rapidly restored morale and adopted the right tactics to exploit the superior firepower of his UN forces. Ridgway was promoted to the post of UN Commander when MacArthur was sacked in April 1951. The following year he succeeded Eisenhower as commander of NATO forces in Europe, and in 1953 he was appointed US Army chief of staff.

JOSEPH STALIN
(1879-1953)

Born in Georgia as Iosif Vissarionovich Dzhugashvili, Stalin was one of the Bolshevik communist revolutionaries who seized power in Russia in 1917, founding the Soviet Union in 1923. By 1930 Stalin had made himself Soviet dictator and the recognized leader of the communist movement worldwide. When the Soviet Union was invaded by Germany in 1941, Stalin became an ally of Britain and the United States in World War II. After 1945, he led his country into the Cold War confrontation with the Western allies.

SYNGMAN RHEE
(1875-1965)

Korean nationalist Syngman Rhee was 70 years old when Korea was freed from Japanese rule in 1945. He had lived much of his life as an exile in the United States, where he campaigned for Korean independence. Returning to the American occupation zone in Korea, in 1948 he was elected president of the Republic of Korea. Rhee was frequently an embarrassment to the Americans, because of his open contempt for freedom and democracy, and his ruthless methods, including mass killings of suspected communists. Totally dedicated to unifying Korea under his rule, he did his utmost to prevent an armistice agreement in 1953. Rhee ruled South Korea as a police state until 1960, when he was forced to resign in the face of popular protests.

PRESIDENT HARRY S. TRUMAN (1884-1972)

Born in Missouri, Truman was a Democrat senator before being elected US vice-president in 1944. He became president on the death of Franklin D. Roosevelt in April 1945, and was re-elected in 1948. Although Truman committed the United States to oppose the spread of communism worldwide (the 'Truman Doctrine' of 1947), he was attacked by Republicans for allegedly permitting the communist takeover of China in 1949. He did not hesitate to order US military intervention in Korea, but remained determined to limit the scope of the war as far as possible. He did not stand for re-election in 1952.

GENERAL JAMES VAN FLEET (1892-1992)

Born in New Jersey, Van Fleet rose to the rank of major-general during the fighting in Europe in World War II. In 1948-9, as head of the US military mission in Greece, he played a key role in suppressing a communist guerrilla movement. Replacing General Ridgway as commander of Eighth Army in April 1951, he proved an able general, and worked hard to strengthen the South Korean army. He was unhappy, however, with the refusal of his superiors to allow a full-scale offensive to win the war. In February 1953 he gave up his command and became an outspoken critic of American government policy on Korea.

GENERAL WALTON H. WALKER (1889-1950)

Born in Texas, General Walker was in command of US Eighth Army in Japan when the Korean War began. In command of US and South Korean army forces in Korea from July 1950, Walker succeeded in rallying his men and defending the Pusan perimeter. From the Inchon landing onward, Walker commanded Eighth Army but not X Corps. He reluctantly obeyed MacArthur's orders to advance towards the Yalu River in November 1950 and did his best to organize the subsequent withdrawal. He died after a road accident on 23 December 1950.

SIGNIFICANT DATES

1910
Korea is taken over by Japan.

1931
The Japanese occupy Manchuria.

1937
Japan goes to war with China, occupying much of the country.

1939-41
Japan and the Soviet Union fight a border war.

7 DECEMBER 1941
Japanese attack on the US base at Pearl Harbor begins World War II in the Pacific.

6 AUGUST 1945
The United States drops an atom bomb on the Japanese city of Hiroshima.

8 AUGUST 1945
The Soviet Union declares war on Japan and invades Manchuria.

15 AUGUST 1945
Japan surrenders; the United States proposes dividing Korea into two occupation zones, north and south of the 38th parallel.

8 SEPTEMBER 1945
American troops arrive at Inchon to begin the occupation of Korea south of the 38th parallel.

MARCH 1947
President Truman commits the United States to blocking the spread of communism worldwide (the 'Truman doctrine').

AUGUST 1948
The Republic of Korea is proclaimed in South Korea, led by Syngman Rhee.

SEPTEMBER 1948
The Democratic People's Republic of Korea is proclaimed in North Korea, led by Kim Il-sung.

NOVEMBER 1948
A guerrilla uprising against Rhee's rule begins on Cheju-do Island.

DECEMBER 1948
Soviet troops pull out of North Korea.

MAY 1949
Beginning of border clashes between North and South Korean forces.

JUNE 1949
US troops leave South Korea.

25 JUNE 1950
North Korean forces invade South Korea.

27 JUNE 1950
UN resolution calls for collective military action in defence of South Korea.

1 JULY 1950
First US troops arrive in South Korea to fight against the North.

7 JULY 1950
General Douglas MacArthur is appointed UN Commander in Korea.

20 JULY 1950
The key city of Taejon falls to the North Korean army.

AUGUST 1950
The Eighth Army struggles to hold a defensive perimeter around the port of Pusan.

28 AUGUST 1950
First British troops arrive in Korea.

15-28 SEPTEMBER 1950
UN forces carry out landings at Inchon and retake Seoul.

1 OCTOBER 1950
South Korean troops cross the 38th parallel into North Korea.

2 OCTOBER 1950
China warns that it will intervene militarily if US forces enter North Korea.

12 OCTOBER 1950
The Eighth Army occupies the North Korean capital, Pyongyang.

19 OCTOBER 1950
Chinese 'Volunteers' begin to filter into North Korea.

25 OCTOBER 1950
First clashes between UN forces and Chinese soldiers.

26 OCTOBER 1950
US Marines land at the port of Wonsan; South Korean units reach the Yalu River, the border between North Korea and China.

6 NOVEMBER 1950
Chinese Volunteers break off fighting with UN forces.

24 NOVEMBER 1950
MacArthur launches a 'final offensive' to the Yalu River.

28 NOVEMBER 1950
Eighth Army withdraws under heavy attack by Chinese and North Korean troops.

30 NOVEMBER 1950
President Truman indicates publicly that the use of atom bombs in Korea is not ruled out.

DECEMBER 1950
British Prime Minister Clement Attlee begins talks with Truman in Washington, opposing the use of atom bombs.

5 DECEMBER 1950
Pyongyang is abandoned to the communists as UN forces retreat to the 38th parallel.

11 DECEMBER 1950
Marines complete a fighting withdrawal from the Chosin Reservoir to the port of Hungnam.

16 DECEMBER 1950
President Truman declares a state of emergency in the United States.

23 DECEMBER 1950
Death of General Walker, commander of Eighth Army; he is replaced by General Matthew Ridgway.

24 DECEMBER 1950
Last UN forces are evacuated from North Korea by sea.

1-15 JANUARY 1951
A renewed communist offensive drives the UN forces back south of Seoul.

25 JANUARY-21 APRIL 1951
UN counter-offensive (the 'meatgrinder') drives the communist forces back to around the 38th parallel.

11 APRIL 1951
President Truman dismisses General MacArthur from all his commands; General Ridgway is appointed UN Commander.

22 APRIL 1951
New Chinese and North Korean offensive leads to heavy fighting on the Imjin River.

29 APRIL 1951
Communist advance halts on the outskirts of Seoul.

16-21 MAY 1951
Renewed communist offensive fails.

10 JULY 1951
Ceasefire negotiations begin at Kaesong.

23 AUGUST 1951
Negotiations are suspended after communist allegations of UN attacks on the talks zone.

AUGUST-OCTOBER 1951
Heavy fighting as UN forces push the front line northward.

25 OCTOBER 1951
Ceasefire talks begin again at Panmunjon.

27 NOVEMBER 1951
Both sides agree in principle on a ceasefire along the current line separating the two armies.

JANUARY 1952
Operation Ratkiller achieves suppression of most guerrilla activity in South Korea.

17 FEBRUARY 1952
Agreement reached for a peace conference to be held after a ceasefire.

19 APRIL 1952
Ceasefire talks stall over issue of repatriation of prisoners of war.

12 MAY 1952
General Mark Clark replaces Ridgway as UN Commander.

MAY 1952
Communist POWs stage revolt on Koje Island.

23 JUNE 1952
UN air attacks destroy the Supung dam and three other hydroelectric dams in North Korea.

20 JANUARY 1953
Dwight D. Eisenhower is inaugurated as US President.

5 MARCH 1953
Death of Soviet dictator Joseph Stalin.

16 APRIL 1953
Beginning of battle for Pork Chop Hill.

26 APRIL 1953
Ceasefire talks resume in earnest.

13-16 MAY 1953
UN air attacks destroy irrigation dams in North Korea.

18 JUNE 1953
Syngman Rhee releases Korean POWs in effort to sabotage ceasefire talks.

JUNE-JULY 1953
Chinese offensives lead to heavy fighting along the Main Line of Resistance.

27 JULY 1953
Ceasefire agreement is signed.

APRIL-JUNE 1954
Geneva Conference fails to achieve agreement on a peace treaty and reunification of Korea.

1960
Syngman Rhee resigns after popular protests against his rule.

1988
South Korea becomes a multi-party democracy.

1991
South Korea and North Korea admitted to the United Nations.

1994
Death of Kim Il-sung; he is succeeded by his son, Kim Jong-il.

2000
South Korean President Kim Dae-jong visits North Korea.

2003
President George W. Bush lists North Korea among a number of 'rogue states' that he considers a threat to world security, and warns that the US will not permit the country to develop a nuclear capabilty.

STATISTICS CONCERNING COMBATANT NATIONS

Australia

Supplied two infantry battalions, nine naval vessels, a fighter squadron and a transport squadron.

Military personnel served in Korea	17,164

Casualties:

Killed or missing in action	411
Wounded	1,216
POWs	21

Belgium

Supplied one infantry battalion.

Military personnel served in Korea	3,498

Casualties:

Killed or missing in action	106
Wounded	336
POWs	1

Britain

Supplied two infantry brigades and approximately 50 naval vessels.

Military personnel served in Korea	60,000

Casualties:

Killed or missing in action	1,078
Wounded	2,533
POWs	766

Canada

Supplied an infantry brigade, eight naval vessels, and a squadron of transport aircraft.

Military personnel served in Korea	27,000

Casualties:

Killed or missing in action	344
Wounded	1,212
POWs	12

China

Casualties:

Killed or missing in action (estimate)	1,000,000

Colombia

Supplied an infantry battalion and six naval vessels.

Military personnel served in Korea	6,200

Casualties:

Killed or missing in action	191
Wounded	448
POWs	29

Ethiopia

Supplied an infantry battalion.

Military personnel served in Korea	3,518

Casualties:

Killed in action	121
Wounded	536

France

Supplied an infantry battalion and a naval vessel.

Military personnel served in Korea	4,000

Casualties:

Killed or missing in action	281
Wounded	1,008
POWs	11

Greece

Supplied an infantry battalion and transport aircraft.

Military personnel served in Korea	5,000

Casualties:

Killed or missing in action	194
Wounded	543
POWs	1

Luxembourg

Supplied a rifle company.

Military personnel served in Korea	89

Casualties:

Killed or missing in action	2
Wounded	13

Netherlands

Supplied an infantry battalion and six naval vessels.

Military personnel served in Korea	5,300

Casualties:

Killed or missing in action	123
Wounded	645

New Zealand

Supplied an artillery regiment and four naval vessels.

Military personnel served in Korea	4,500

Casualties:

Killed in action	34
Wounded	79
POWs	1

North Korea
Military casualties:
Killed or missing in action	500,000
Civilian deaths (estimate)	2,000,000

Philippines
Supplied a battalion combat team.
Military personnel served in Korea	7,420

Casualties:
Killed or missing in action	179
Wounded	299
POWs	40

South Africa
Supplied one fighter aircraft squadron.
Military personnel served in Korea	811

Casualties:
Killed in action	20
Wounded	16
POWs	6

South Korea
Military casualties:
Killed or missing in action	415,004
Wounded	1,312,836
POWs	85,000

Civilian deaths
(estimates) 660,000–1,000,000

Thailand
Supplied an infantry battalion, four naval vessels, and transport aircraft.
Military personnel served in Korea	6,500

Casualties:
Killed or missing in action	134
Wounded	1,139

Turkey
Supplied a brigade group.
Military personnel served in Korea	15,000

Casualties:
Killed or missing in action	1,148
Wounded	2,068
POWs	219

United States
Total US military personnel who served in Korea 1950-3	1,789,000

Casualties:
Combat deaths	33,686 *
US Army	27,728
US Marines	4,268
US Air Force	1,198
US Navy	492
Wounded	103,284
Unaccounted for	8,176
POWs	7,245

(of whom 2,806 died, included in figure for combat deaths)

*A figure of over 54,000 is sometimes given for US dead in the Korean War, but this higher figure includes all US military deaths worldwide during the Korean War period. There were also 2,830 US non-battle deaths in Korea, making total US deaths in the Korean theatre 36,516.

US air operations in Korea:
US Navy	275,912 sorties
USAF	1,325,000 sorties

Estimated 1,500 enemy aircraft shot down

GLOSSARY

38th parallel Line of latitude 38 degrees north of the equator, this was the original dividing line between North and South Korea.

air strike Attack by aircraft using bombs, missiles, rockets or guns.

amphibious operation Military operation in which troops transported by sea make a landing in enemy-held territory.

arbitrary Something done or chosen for no particular reason.

armistice An agreement between two sides in a war to stop fighting temporarily, pending peace negotiations.

atom bomb An extremely powerful bomb in which the explosion is caused by splitting atoms; the weapon was first made and used by the United States in 1945. In addition to causing immediate massive destruction, it releases deadly long-term radiation, making it a 'doomsday' weapon of last resort.

authoritarian A government or ruler exercising power in a strict way with no regard for individual freedom.

battalion An army formation made up of several companies (see below).

blockade To stop people and goods from going in or out of a town, port or country.

boycott To refuse to take part in something or to trade with someone.

brigade A large army formation made up of several battalions or regiments.

capitalism Economic system based on a free market and private ownership of land and industry.

ceasefire Another word for an armistice (see above).

charter The charter of the UN is the document that sets out what the organization is for, and how and when it is supposed to act.

chief of staff The senior officer in one of a country's armed forces.

civilians People not in the armed forces.

coalition A government in which more than one political party takes part.

Cold War The armed confrontation between the United States and its allies on one side and the Soviet Union and its allies on the other, which lasted from the late 1940s to the 1980s. It stopped short of a full-blown 'hot war' out of fear of the destructive effects of nuclear bombs and their radioactivity.

collaborate To co-operate, but in wartime used as a critical term meaning that a person has helped the enemy forces occupying his or her country.

colony A country ruled by a foreign power as part of its empire.

communism A political and economic system first established in the Soviet Union and which then spread to many other countries; it involved rule by a single political party and control of industry and agriculture by the state.

company In an army, a company is a unit made up of a number of platoons.

corps A grouping of army formations brought together for a specific purpose in a war – for example, to fight in one area of a front line.

CPV Chinese People's Volunteers – name given to the Chinese forces in the Korean War.

defensive perimeter A line around a city or other important place that an army sets out to hold against attacking enemy forces.

delegation A group of people who represent their side in negotiations.

demilitarized zone An area in which no soldiers or weapons are allowed to be stationed.

democracy Political system in which people freely elect their rulers.

Democrat A member of one of the United States' two major political parties (see also Republican).

demoralized Short of confidence and fighting spirit.

dictator A ruler who has absolute power over the people in his country.

division An army grouping similar to a corps (see above) but smaller – there are typically two divisions to a corps.

DMZ Demilitarized zone (see above).

dynasty A succession of kings, queens or emperors belonging to the same family.

empire A number of nations ruled by a single dominant power.

escalate To make a conflict more intense.

Geneva Convention An international agreement on how wars should be fought, including rules for the treatment of prisoners of war.

guerrilla war War waged by lightly armed fighters who are not members of a regular army.

imperialists Countries that dominate and exploit other countries as part of an empire.

indoctrination The process of drumming a set of beliefs into someone.

intelligence-gathering Finding out information about an enemy's forces or plans.

military personnel Members of the armed forces – soldiers, sailors, airmen etc.

napalm Burning petrol used as a weapon, often dropped in bombs from aircraft.

nationalist In Korea, someone who wanted the country to be independent and united.

negotiations Talks aimed at reaching agreement on certain issues.

neutrality pact An agreement not to take part in a war.

NKPA North Korean People's Army.

no man's land The area between the front lines of two armies confronting one another.

outflank To advance around the side of an enemy position.

perimeter The outer boundary of an area.

platoon A small unit of soldiers - several platoons make up a company.

police state State in which the police are used ruthlessly to suppress all political opposition.

propaganda Information (sometimes false) given out by a government or organization in order to persuade people of the rightness of its own cause and beliefs, and of the wrongness of its enemies'.

regime Government or system of government.

regiment A large permanent army formation.

repatriation Sending someone back to their country of origin.

Republican A member of one of the United States' two major political parties (see also Democrat).

resolution A formal proposal to be voted on.

reunification Joining together something that has been divided.

ROK Republic of Korea, usually known as South Korea.

sabotage Deliberate damage to or destruction of machinery, railway lines, etc.

Security Council Part of the United Nations entrusted with maintaining international peace and security; in 1950 the five permanent members of the Security Council were Britain, France, the Soviet Union, the USA and Nationalist China, and the six non-permanent members (serving for two years) were Cuba, Egypt, Ecuador, India, Norway and Yugoslavia.

Soviet Union The communist state which, until 1991, ruled a large area of Europe and Asia, including Russia, Ukraine, and Belorussia.

supply line Route along which weapons, fuel, ammunition and food are brought to an army.

trusteeship In international affairs, an arrangement under which one country runs another for a limited period, until it is deemed fit to govern itself.

unification Joining together something that has been divided.

United Nations Organization Organization established in 1945 to promote world peace and co-operation between states.

veto The right to reject or block an action or proposal.

RECOMMENDED BOOKS

There are many general histories of the Korean War (mostly imaginatively titled!), the best of which are listed below. While they may contain more information than younger readers can digest in their entirety, using the contents page or index of each book is a good way of finding out more about a particular battle or aspect of the war.
Brian Catchpole, *The Korean War*, Constable 2000.

Jon Halliday and Bruce Cumings, *Korea: The Unknown War*, Penguin 1990 (an account highly critical of the United States).

Max Hastings, *The Korean War*, Pan 1988

Michael Hickey, *The Korean War: The West Confronts Communism 1950-53*, John Murray 1999.

Burton I. Kaufman, *The Korean Conflict*, Greenwood Press 1999 (a source book giving overviews of the subject from various angles, followed by a discussion of source material of all sorts, from original documents to films).

Carter Malkasian, *The Korean War 1950-53*, Fitzroy Dearborn 2001 (a short account of the war).

Carter Smith, *The Korean War*, Silver Burdett Press 1991 (one of the 'Turning Points in American History' series for younger readers).

Richard Conrad Stein, *The Korean War 'The Forgotten War'*, Enslow Publishers 1994 (part of the 'American War Series').

Also of interest are:
Ann Gaines, *Douglas MacArthur: Brilliant General, Controversial Leader*, Enslow Publishers 2001 (written for children aged 10 and over, this illustrated title is part of the 'Historical American Biographies' series).

Donald Knox, *The Korean War: Pusan to Chosin: An Oral History*, Harcourt 1985 (the story of the war as told by those who fought in it).

Richard Leckie, *March to Glory*, Simon & Schuster 2002 (tells the dramatic story of the US Marines at the Chosin Reservoir).

Ivan Rendall, *Rolling Thunder: Jet Combat from World War II to the Gulf War*, New York 1997 (has a good chapter on the air war in Korea).

Novels set in the Korean War include:
W.E.B. Griffen, *Under Fire*, Jove Books 2003
W.E.B. Griffen, *Retreat, Hell!*, Putnam's 2004

SOURCES OF QUOTATIONS

Korea: The Unknown War, Jon Halliday and Bruce Cumings, Penguin, London 1990.

Office of the Press Secretary, The White House, October 2003.

Rethinking the Korean War, William Stueck, Princeton University Press, Princeton 2002.

The Guardian newspaper, London and Manchester.

The Korean War, Brian Catchpole, Constable, London 2000.

The Korean War, Michael Hickey, John Murray, London 1999.

The War in Korea, Matthew B. Ridgway, Barrie & Rockliff, London 1967.

War in Peace magazine, London 1983.

RECOMMENDED FILMS

Korea has certainly been 'the Forgotten War' as far as filmmakers are concerned. There are no movies that can be unreservedly recommended as giving a true impression of the conflict.

M.A.S.H. (1970) is the only well-known film set in the Korean War. However, it was made during the Vietnam War, and the attitudes expressed in it are much more typical of that conflict than of Korea. There is also a spin-off TV series of the same name. Both are based on Richard Hooker's comic novel for an adult audience, *M*A*S*H: A Novel About Three Army Doctors.*

The Manchurian Candidate (1962) is a thriller based on the idea of American prisoners of war in Korea being 'brainwashed' so that they act as communist agents after their return to the US.

The *Sergeant Bilko* black-and-white TV comedy series perhaps gives some impression of the kind of peacetime US Army that found it hard to adapt to war in Korea.

RECOMMENDED WEBSITES

http://korea50.army.mil/
This is a US Army website with biographies, maps, factsheets and eyewitness accounts of the war from veterans.

www.usni.org
This US Naval Institute site has a Korean War interactive timeline, with animated maps.

www.militaryhistory.about.com
This has some interesting material on the Korean War and good links.

www.nps.gov/kwvm
A website devoted to the Korean War Veterans Memorial in Washington D.C.

Note to parents and teachers

Every effort has been made by the publishers to ensure that these websites are suitable for children; that they are of the highest educational value; and that they contain no inappropriate or offensive material. However, because of the nature of the Internet, it is impossible to guarantee that the contents of these sites will not be altered. We strongly advise that Internet access is supervised by a responsible adult.

PLACES TO VISIT

The Korean War Veterans Memorial
900 Ohio Drive, SW
Washington D.C. 20024
USA
The Korean War Veterans Memorial in Washington D.C. is striking. It consists of 19 individual statues representing a military unit on patrol, a 'wall of faces' which carries depictions of more than 2,000 serving personnel taken from photographs of servicemen and women who participated in the conflict, a United Nations wall that lists the countries that provided troops, support or supplies to South Korea, and a Pool of Remembrance where an inscription reads 'Our nation honors her sons and daughters who answered the call to defend a country they never knew and a people they never met'.

Korean War Museum
Yongsan-gu
Seoul
South Korea
This museum in the city of Seoul covers the military history of the country, but most of the exhibits are devoted to the Korean War of 1950-3. The park surrounding the museum is filled with displays of aircraft, tanks and artillery pieces dating from the time of the conflict.

INDEX